MW00913797

The
Italian
Americans

By Catherine M. Petrini

Lucent Books, 10911 Technology Place, San Diego, CA 92127

Other books in the Immigrants in America series:

The Chinese Americans
The Cuban Americans
The Vietnamese Americans
The Russian Americans

Library of Congress Cataloging-in-Publication Data

Petrini, Catherine M.
  The Italian Americans / by Catherine M. Petrini
    p. cm. — (Immigrants in America)
Includes bibliographical references (p.) and index.
Summary: Reviews the reasons why millions of Italians have immigrated to America, what their passage was like, the kinds of jobs most found, communities they formed, and the prejudice they faced.
  ISBN 1-56006-882-5 (hardback : alk. paper)
1. Italian Americans—History—Juvenile literature. 2. Immigrants—United States—History—Juvenile literature. 3. United States—Emigration and immigration—History—Juvenile literature. 4. Italy—Emigration and immigration—History—Juvenile literature.
[1. Italian Americans—History. 2. Immigrants. 3. United States—Emigration and immigration. 4. Italy—Emigration and immigration.]
I.Title. II. Series.
  E184.I8 P48 2002
  305.851073—dc21

2001002428

Printed in the USA

Contents

FOREWORD

Immigrants have come to America at different times, for different reasons, and from many different places. They leave their homelands to escape religious and political persecution, poverty, war, famine, and countless other hardships. The journey is rarely easy. Sometimes, it entails a long and hazardous ocean voyage. Other times, it follows a circuitous route through refugee camps and foreign countries. At the turn of the twentieth century, for instance, Italian peasants, fleeing poverty, boarded steamships bound for New York, Boston, and other eastern seaports. And during the 1970s and 1980s, Vietnamese men, women, and children, victims of a devastating war, began arriving at refugee camps in Arkansas, Pennsylvania, Florida, and California, en route to establishing new lives in the United States.

Whatever the circumstances surrounding their departure, the immigrants' journey is always made more difficult by the knowledge that they leave behind family, friends, and a familiar way of life. Despite this, immigrants continue to come to America because, for many, the United States represents something they could not find at home: freedom and opportunity for themselves and their children.

No matter what their reasons for emigrating, where they have come from, or when they left, once here, nearly all immigrants face considerable challenges in adapting and making the United States

their new home. Language barriers, unfamiliar surroundings, and sometimes hostile neighbors make it difficult for immigrants to assimilate into American society. Some Vietnamese, for instance, could not read or write in their native tongue when they arrived in the United States. This heightened their struggle to communicate with employers who demanded they be literate in English, a language vastly different from their own. Likewise, Irish immigrant school children in Boston faced classmates who teased and belittled their lilting accent. Immigrants from Russia often felt isolated, having settled in areas of the United States where they had no access to traditional Russian foods. Similarly, Italian families, used to certain wines and spices, rarely shopped or traveled outside of New York's Little Italy, a self-contained community cut off from the rest of the city.

Even when first-generation immigrants do successfully settle into life in the United States, their children, born in America, often have different values and are influenced more by their country of birth than their parents' traditions. Children want to be a part of the American culture and usually welcome American ideals, beliefs, and styles. As they become more Americanized—adopting western dating habits and fashions, for instance—they tend to cast aside or even actively reject the traditions embraced by their parents. Assimilation, then, often becomes an ideological dispute that creates conflict among immigrants of every ethnicity. Whether Chinese, Italian, Russian, or Vietnamese, young people battle their elders for respect, individuality, and freedom, issues that often would not have come up in their homeland. And no matter how tightly the first generations hold onto their traditions, in the end, it is usually the young people who decide what to keep and what to discard.

The Immigrants in America series fully examines the immigrant experience. Each book in the series discusses why the immigrants left their homeland, what the journey to America was like, what they experienced when they arrived, and the challenges of assimilation. Each volume includes discussion of triumph and tragedy, contributions and influences, history and the future. Fully documented primary and secondary source quotations enliven the text. Sidebars highlight interesting events and personalities. Annotated bibliographies offer ideas for additional research. Each book in this dynamic series provides students with a wealth of information as well as launching points for further discussion.

A New Odyssey

In 1909, on the steerage-class deck of a steamship crossing the Atlantic Ocean, Rosalina Ambrosini DeRiggi gave birth to her sixth child, Michael. He was her fourth surviving child and the first of his family to be born away from Cicciano, a village in the hills outside Naples in southern Italy. To Rosalina (soon known as Rose) and her husband, Giovanni (John), baby "Micky" was a living symbol of the family's future in a new land.

The DeRiggis were among millions of Italians who immigrated to America during the peak Italian immigration period. Between 1880 and 1930, more than 4.5 million Italians entered the United States, more than any other ethnic group at the time. The numbers were so high that the mayor of one Italian town reportedly commented on the mass migration when he greeted the visiting prime minister, saying, "I welcome you in the name of five thousand inhabitants of this town, three thousand of whom are in America and the other two thousand preparing to go."[1]

A Flood of Arrivals

According to U.S. Immigration and Naturalization Service figures, more than 5.4 million Italians immigrated to the United States between 1820 and 1998, with most of them coming between 1892 and 1924, the so-called Ellis Island years. In 1892, with U.S. companies hungry for labor, Ellis Island, off the coast of New York City, opened its gates as a primary entrance port for immigration. There were other U.S. entry points, but most Italian immigrants arrived through Ellis Island. During its peak year, 1907, the island processed a million arrivals from dozens of foreign nations. Numbers for all immigrants, including Italians, began to decline during World War I (1914 to 1918), however, because travel became difficult during the war,

and because Congress imposed tight new restrictions on the numbers of foreign-born people allowed into the country. In 1924, even tougher quotas for southern Europeans virtually dammed the flood of arrivals from Italy. By then, however, those already in the United States were firmly entrenched in their new lives.

Today, 15 million Americans claim Italian ancestry, making Italian Americans the nation's fifth largest ethnic group. The U.S. Census Bureau puts the figure higher, saying

This family, like most Italian immigrants, passed through Ellis Island upon arriving in the United States.

that one out of ten Americans has some Italian ancestry, bringing the total number of Americans of Italian descent to 26 million. Emigration from Italy continues even today, although in much smaller numbers.

Originally, most Italian immigrants settled in the industrialized regions along the East Coast. Today, even though Italian Americans live in every state, New York leads the country in the number of Italian American residents with 2.9 million, almost twice as many as any other state. Other states with high Italian American populations include California and New Jersey, each with 1.5 million residents; Pennsylvania, with 1.4 million; Massachusetts, with 845,000; Connecticut, with 630,000; and Rhode Island, with 200,000. The five U.S. cities with the highest Italian American populations are New York, Philadelphia, Chicago, Boston, and Pittsburgh.

Enriching the Culture

Numbers, though, do not tell the whole story. Italian immigrants like Rose and John De-

Many early Italian immigrants settled in New York City.

Riggi brought with them the language, folklore, art forms, traditions, and cuisine of their homeland. In the process, they changed and enriched American culture forever. Today, Americans of all ancestries eat such Italian specialties as pizza and lasagna; even Barrow, Alaska, a town 350 miles above the Arctic Circle, boasts a pizza parlor. From renowned tenor Enrico Caruso, whose performances raised money for the United States and its allies during World War I, to crooner and actor Frank Sinatra, to pop icon Madonna (whose last name is Ciccone), Italian immigrants and their descendants have entertained the world and transformed the sound of American music. Superstar athletes such as baseball legend Joe DiMaggio and Olympic gymnast Mary Lou Retton (Ret-toni) also have Italian roots. Francis Ford Coppola, Penny Marshall (Marscharelli), and other Italian American film directors craft images on movie screens. Italian Americans teach, hold political office, cure illnesses, run major corporations and small family businesses, and are active in religious organizations. They build railroads, mine coal, and pilot airplanes. They invented the radio, the ice cream cone, and the coffee maker.

In short, Italian immigrants and their descendants live in every part of the country and make contributions in every field of endeavor. From Barrow, Alaska, to Baton Rouge, Louisiana, from Boston, Massachusetts, to Bakersfield, California, the sons and daughters of Italy have influenced every aspect of American life.

CHAPTER ONE

Roots of Mass Migration

The reasons why millions of people chose to uproot their families during the peak immigration years are grounded in poverty, repression, and a sense of powerlessness. These had become a way of life for rural Italians, especially in the southern part of Italy. The political situation in the Italian provinces lay at the root of the people's despair.

A Nation Divided

In the early part of the nineteenth century, the period just before the mass migration, Italy existed not as one country but as a collection of eight separate provinces. All but one province were under the foreign rule of Spain or Austria or were controlled by the Catholic Church. Only the kingdom of Sardinia was independent. This kingdom consisted of the island of Sardinia, off the northwestern coast, and the geographical region of the mainland known as the Piedmont, in Italy's northwest corner, near France. Not even the Italian language was unified; the dialects spoken in the various parts of Italy were so different that residents of the various regions could not understand each other.

The poorest part of Italy, was popularly called the Mezzogiorno. the region south of Rome. Although northern Italy was wealthy and industrial, in the south—especially on the island of Sicily—most Italians lived in poverty. Most farmed land they did not own and suffered under the indifference of rich overseers and landowners. Under the dominion of the Spanish Bourbon dynasty, which ruled the south, the *contadini* (peasants) had little hope of improving their lives or the lives of their children. In some families it was understood that "only the eldest son could marry," says Rudolph J. Vecoli in an unpublished dissertation, because only one son could inherit enough to support a family. At the same time, "the family could usually provide a dowry for only one daughter."[2] Other sons and daughters were forced to remain unmarried, sometimes joining the priesthood or becoming nuns.

The *contadini* were not slaves; their employers did not own them. Instead, the peasants earned wages, though usually meager ones, and were free to quit. But their options were few. Other job opportunities did not exist in southern Italy, and few people could read and write. Thus, the poorest laborers continued to toil for the rich landowners, frequently under armed guard to ensure that they worked efficiently and did not loaf. Travel was also strictly limited for the peasants. From the Bourbons' point of view, isolating villages from each other helped keep people ignorant and therefore unlikely to disrupt the status quo.

This system continued for decades. The *contadini* had little exposure to other places

Naples, Italy (pictured), was the most important city in the Mezzogiorno, an area south of Rome that was poor and whose inhabitants labored for rich landowners.

or lifestyles. And illiteracy and language differences from one place to another helped quash the spread of information. The *contadini* feared the wrath of both their employers and the government, so most did as they were told. They were too poor to do otherwise. Traveling required money, and few families had any to spare for anything beyond food and shelter.

Reawakening the Spirit of Italy

Between 1815 and 1861, the Italian provinces experienced a period of turmoil that raised the peasants' hopes. This was the time of *risorgimento* (resurgence or reawakening), named after the battle cry of a revolution that aimed to force out foreign rulers, lessen control by the Catholic Church, and unite the Italian provinces. The revolution

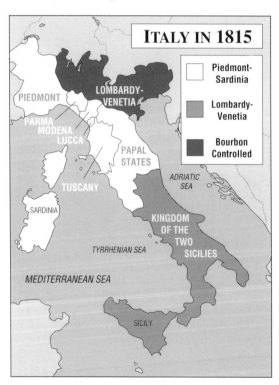

ITALY IN 1815

Piedmont-Sardinia

Lombardy-Venetia

Bourbon Controlled

PIEDMONT

LOMBARDY-VENETIA

PARMA
MODENA
LUCCA

PAPAL STATES

TUSCANY

ADRIATIC SEA

SARDINIA

KINGDOM OF THE TWO SICILIES

TYRRHENIAN SEA

MEDITERRANEAN SEA

SICILY

did not take the form of a single, unified movement at first. Instead, it swelled and ebbed in different regions in a series of mostly unsuccessful, minor uprisings. Gradually, though, the ideas of unity and independence took hold.

Because the independent kingdom of Sardinia had its capital in the Piedmontese city of Turin, the revolution grew out of the north, and the leaders of risorgimento were all northerners. Only northerners had the education, the political savvy, and the resources to stage a grand-scale insurrection. Their goal was to fold the other provinces into the kingdom of Sardinia, which would then become the new country of Italy.

At first, the southern peasants viewed risorgimento with suspicion. Most were afraid to challenge the Catholic Church. Some balked at following the lead of northerners. Others had no interest in politics and were skeptical about claims that changing their government would change their fortunes for the better. Besides, the idea of a unified Italy seemed alien to them; they did not think of themselves as Italians but as residents of their villages or provinces. Some peasants, however, eventually came to support risorgimento in hopes that the rule of Italy by Italians would give them more control over their own lives. In particular, they clung to the promises of revolutionary leaders who assured them that in the new, unified Italy, land would be available to all. Many of the poorest people, though, remained passive. The struggle to survive took all their time and resources; they had no energy left to contribute to the cause.

Winning the South

By 1859, much of Italy had been unified under Sardinian king Victor Emmanuel II. However, the Catholic Church, run by the Vatican, still ruled a portion of central Italy, including Rome, and the Spanish Bourbon dynasty controlled the Mezzogiorno. Victor Emmanuel set his sights on Sicily, at the farthest tip of the Mezzogiorno. With dominion over Sicily, he would control both ends of Italy, making him too powerful for anyone else to oppose for long. To achieve his ends, Victor Emmanuel asked Piedmontese general Giuseppe Garibaldi to annex Sicily for his expanding kingdom. Garibaldi raised a volunteer army of one thousand and sailed south.

Sicily, an island at the toe of the boot-shaped peninsula that is Italy, was and remains the nation's poorest region. It was also the most superstitious. The Sicilian peasants especially feared angering their priests by accepting a new regime with eventual ambitions that included overthrowing the Vatican's control of Rome. But because of their crushing poverty, Sicilians also longed more desperately for change than did people in other parts of the south, and they hated the Bourbon rulers more passionately. Garibaldi won their hearts with his charisma and his fervor for the cause, and the Sicilians joined forces with his army.

By August, Garibaldi's forces had overthrown the Spanish Bourbon rulers and taken Sicily. Garibaldi declared himself dictator of Sicily and began pushing his way up the peninsula, conquering lands ruled by Spain and the church. He stopped his drive only when Victor Emmanuel sent his own army to prevent Garibaldi from taking the city of Rome, the seat of the Vatican's remaining power. Victor Emmanuel refrained from an-

King Victor Emmanuel II set out to control southern Italy by taking the island of Sicily.

nexing Rome because he knew he had to move slowly in stripping the church of its power if he wanted to keep the support of his subjects, almost all of whom were Catholic. In addition, the king feared Garibaldi's popularity. He didn't want his general becoming more powerful than he was himself.

Victor Emmanuel needn't have worried. Garibaldi was at that time a loyal general who craved a unified nation, not personal power. Garibaldi avoided a fight with the king's troops by giving Victor Emmanuel the conquered lands, including Sicily and the rest of the Mezzogiorno. In March 1861, the king declared all the annexed possessions to be part of a newly created kingdom of Italy. By 1866, only Rome remained independent.

Disillusionment and Despair

Southern peasants soon found their hopes for self-rule dashed. They had expected some

ITALY IN 1861

GERMAN CONFEDERATION

SWITZERLAND

AUSTRIAN EMPIRE

FRANCE

Turin
PIEDMONT
Milan
LOMBARDY
Venice
Trieste

LIGURIA
EMILIA

Nice
Genoa
ROMAGNA

Florence

TUSCANY
Ancona

OTTOMAN EMPIRE

CORSICA
UMBRIA
THE MARCHES
DALMATIA

PAPAL STATES
ADRIATIC SEA

Rome

Sassari

Gaeta
Foggia
Bari
APULIA
BASILICATA

SARDINIA
TYRRHENIAN SEA
Naples

Salerno
Brindisi

Cagliari
Potenza

Sapri

Cosenza

Palermo
Calatafimi
Messina
CALABRIA
Milazzo
Reggio

TUNISIA

Marsala
SICILY
Catania

Girgenti

MEDITERRANEAN SEA

MALTA

form of regional government. But the revolution only passed the reins of power from foreign rulers to the northern Italian gentry. The new northern government was no more sympathetic to the plight of the *contadini* than the Bourbons had been. The promised redistribution of land to the poor never materialized; Victor Emmanuel chose instead to raise money by selling the acquired properties to the already-wealthy landowners. He also imposed new taxes on the south. Only 2 percent of Italy's people could vote, and they all lived in the northern provinces. As a result, the *contadini* had no recourse against Victor Emmanuel or his laws. Instead of seeing their lives improve, the southern peasants remained as impoverished as ever.

Of the peasants' growing disillusionment, author Gay Talese writes, "The unification of Italy . . . had been forced upon the south by the north, by the promoters of the Risorgimento, and since then the ruling government of Italy . . . had brought to the south nothing but worsening poverty and the necessity of emigration. It had driven out the Bourbons, deglorified the capital city of Naples, and replaced it with nothing."[3]

Garibaldi himself was one of the sharpest critics of the new Italy. "It is a different Italy than I had dreamed of all my life," he said in 1882, "not this miserable, poverty-stricken, humiliated Italy we see now, governed by the dregs of the nation."[4]

Both the revolutionary leaders who had believed and reiterated Victor Emmanuel's promises and the *contadini* felt betrayed and disillusioned. During the revolution, Garibaldi had whipped up the peasants' fervor for change. Now they refused to be kept down. When the king issued a new conscription law, forcing all men to enter the military at age seventeen (except those who could afford to purchase exemptions), the frustrated peasants became angry. They rebelled violently in southern cities and villages. Victor Emmanuel, anxious to show the world that he was in control, reacted harshly, at one point sending half his army to stop the uprisings.

"Whole villages were burnt to the ground on the mere suspicion that they might be providing food and shelter for rebels," say authors Jerre Mangione and Ben Morreale,

"and any insult to the national flag or to a portrait of King Victor Emmanuel was considered reason enough to shoot the perpetrator."[5] In the Sicilian city of Palermo, authorities arrested more than two thousand men and women. Executions took place in several cities, and the king's military commander ordered troops to seize any man who was of military age or who looked like an assassin.

Life in the New Italy

In 1871, Victor Emmanuel finally annexed Rome and made it his capital. In twelve years, the Sardinian king had gone from ruling 5 million subjects in the north to ruling 21 million throughout the peninsula. Modern Italy was born, but its growing pains were only beginning.

Giuseppe Garibaldi won the fight for Sicily and declared himself dictator of the island.

Booker T. Washington, an American educator and reformer who had been born a slave, toured Italy in 1911 as part of a lengthy European study tour. "The Negro is not the man farthest down," he wrote after seeing the plight of Sicily's poor. "The condition of the coloured farmer in the most backward parts of the Southern States in America . . . is incomparably better than the condition and opportunities of the agricultural population in Sicily."[6] Washington was appalled by the living conditions he witnessed on the island. The *contadini* lived in one-room, windowless hovels, sometimes with sleeping lofts. Floors were earth or stone. Indoor plumbing was unknown; children defecated in the streets. Peasants lit their houses with kerosene lamps. Most homes had ovens, but the poorest people cooked in outdoor ovens cobbled together from piles of stones. Goats, pigs, and chickens often shared living space with a family. Malnutrition was rampant. And few children attended school.

Childhood and Education

The Bourbon rulers had considered education for their Italian subjects to be unnecessary and potentially dangerous. If the peasants learned to read and write, if they learned about the world beyond their villages, their rulers feared, they might try to better their lives. As a rural workforce, the peasants were easier to control if they were kept ignorant. So, schools were scarce before the revolution. Only the wealthy were allowed to educate their children.

After risorgimento, however, the Italian government made elementary school education compulsory, meaning that all children had to attend school until the age of ten. It was part of Victor Emmanuel's promised reforms, a chance for a better life for the Italian people. But the national government was in Rome. Affairs in the villages were handled by local authorities, and rich landowners controlled many of those local governments. They also controlled the police departments. With the support of the police, the landowners managed to ignore any national laws they disliked. Seeing no advantage in educating the poor, and not wanting to spend the money to do so, many local authorities simply neglected to build public schools.

After the revolution, the Italian government made elementary-school education mandatory, but many children did not attend.

In towns that did have schools, many children did not attend. Poor families needed the wages of every able-bodied worker. Gay Talese describes childhood in Maida, a town in southern Italy where his father, Joseph, grew up in a landowning peasant family during the early 1900s. By the age of seven, Joseph worked before school as a tailor's apprentice. In fact, school began late, at nine o'clock, because nearly every boy worked at a job for several hours in the morning, beginning at sunrise. They worked again after school. Joseph's evenings were spent laboring again in the tailor shop, or sometimes on his grandfather's farm, which was short of workers because so many men had been drafted into the Italian army. Joseph, a serious, studious boy with no interest in physical labor, was grateful for the long hours in his uncle's tailor shop, which kept him away from the backbreaking farmwork he hated.

Even for a boy like Joseph, who enjoyed his work at the tailor shop, childhood in southern Italy was bleak by today's standards. "When he was a boy growing up in his village during World War I, there were no games to be played, no opportunities for leisure or relaxation," says Joseph's son. "It was a time and place in which child labor was not only accepted but demanded by the destitute conditions of the day; and my father passed through his adolescent years without knowing what it was like to be young."[7]

Other jobs available for boys as young as eight years old included toiling as *carusi* in the sulfur mines of Sicily. A *caruso* was a boy who hauled the sulfur from deep underground that the men blasted and picked out of the earth. The work was arduous. The sacks of sulfur could weigh as much as seventy-five

Gay Talese, the son of Italian immigrants, tells the story of his father's early life in Maida, Italy.

pounds each, and the bosses expected each boy to make fifty trips up the mine shaft each day.

Most *contadini* then were illiterate and expected their children's lives to be much like their own. Many saw no reason to educate their sons and daughters. In fact, among peasants in the south, children who wanted to remain in school after age ten faced criticism for shirking their duty to help support their families.

Replacing One Tyranny with Another

By 1900, 65 percent of the land in Italy was owned by land barons who lived elsewhere.

Unfair Tax Reform

Under the new laws of a reunified Italy, many peasants who had been considered too poor to pay taxes to the old Bourbon rulers began receiving tax bills. Even worse, southern peasants were taxed unfairly.

To raise money while staying in the good graces of the wealthy landowners, King Victor Emmanuel placed a heavy tax burden on the people who could least afford it. For instance, the new national government levied higher taxes on millers for grinding wheat (a "grist tax") than for grinding corn. That drove up the price of wheat, a staple of southern diets; northern Italians relied instead on corn. In 1884, the tax was repealed. But many millers chose not to lower their prices. They pocketed the extra profits, leaving the peasants no better off than when the tax was in effect.

Taxes on grain were not the only ones the *contadini* found discriminatory. The government charged taxes on mules, which were commonly owned by poor farmworkers. Cows, nearly always the property of rich landowners, were not taxed. Such taxes increased the peasants' dissatisfaction with their lives under the new government and made them more susceptible to tales of an easier life across the ocean.

These landlords charged high rents and paid low wages. For example, most male agricultural laborers in Italy earned sixteen to thirty cents a day around the turn of the twentieth century. The pay scale for women workers was one-half to three-fourths of that. With such low pay, it was nearly impossible for Italians to make enough money to buy anything beyond the most basic necessities.

Land in the south was especially likely to be owned by absentee landlords, who left agents or overseers in charge of their estates. Many overseers knew nothing about farming methods and did not care if they destroyed the soil—and the people who worked it—in the process. All they cared about were short-term profits. According to historians, the overseers' goal, "one that was adopted by the peasants who tilled the fields for them—was to take as much from the soil as possible in the shortest length of time."[8]

Though the overseers worked for the landowners, they were allowed to keep a percentage of the profits they could squeeze from the peasants. So they squeezed as hard as they could. And with their bosses away most of the time, they quickly built power bases of their own. Overseers bullied people with threats and violence, and they used bribes and intimidation to gain enough influence with local police departments and other officials so that no one dared to oppose them. Writer Michael Musmanno describes their methods: "When tenants failed to meet the landlord's demands the agents [overseers] often hired thugs to warn the tenants that if they did not pay up, broken bones could follow. At first, anonymous threats were disregarded, but when tenants fell under nocturnal cudgels [beatings] and their livestock was driven away, others who received similar threats responded with more alacrity [promptness] than they might have to notices from the sheriff."[9]

Those bands of overseers evolved into groups of another kind. Authors Mangione and Morreale write, "Prevalent in Sicily, absentee landlordism spawned a class of notorious overseers known as *gabelloti*. Their rapid rise in society paralleled that of *mafiosi* . . . whose services they [the *gabelloti*] frequently employed to collect unpaid rents or to intimidate sharecroppers into accepting unfair contracts."[10]

Toward the end of the nineteenth century, the word *mafiosi,* which originally had referred simply to people with tough and fiery temperaments, was being used for individuals involved in criminal organizations. The *mafiosi* worked under contract; anyone with enough money could hire them. As the overseers grew richer, they could afford to hire such help themselves, instead of relying on their bosses' budgets. Sometimes the overseers even used the *mafiosi* to intimidate their bosses in order to get better deals for themselves. Many of the *gabelloti* began as landless peasants but eventually became wealthier than the nobles they claimed to serve.

Living off the Land

Most of Italy's population, though, more than 80 percent, worked in agriculture. Typically, they lived in ancient hill towns perched high above farmlands. The towns had been built on the rocky hilltops, or even into the cliffs, for protection against the bands of raiders and the diseases that ravaged the lowlands. This meant the people lived far from the fields, orchards, and vineyards where they worked. Agricultural workers—men, women, and

Most of Italy's residents during the late nineteenth and early twentieth centuries worked in agriculture.

children—spent up to four hours each day trudging to and from their jobs. Often they walked on country roads that in dry weather were choked with dust and in wet weather oozed with mud.

Once the workers reached the fields, they tilled the earth with tools and techniques that hadn't changed in hundreds of years. Booker T. Washington compared the crude wrought-iron hoes he saw in Sicily in 1911 to the primitive tools that slaves had used on American plantations before the U.S. Civil War, half a century earlier.

The soil of southern Italy was thin and rocky. Rain fell at the wrong times of year for farming. Earthquakes, mud slides, and volcanic eruptions were constant threats. Even in the best of times, it was not an easy place to make a living. Between 1870 and 1900, the difficulties multiplied. During that period, the market for Italian agricultural products deteriorated, partly because of government reforms aimed at making it easier for the new Italy to do business with foreign countries. Before the late nineteenth century, for instance, most of the grain that Italians bought was grown in Italy. Victor Emmanuel's new laws, though, made it cheaper for Russia and the United States to sell their grain in Italy, so Italians stopped buying Italian grain. This new rule and others achieved the king's goals of bringing foreign money into Italy and improving his fledgling country's image among other nations. The rules also made life increasingly difficult for Italian farmworkers.

Agricultural developments in other countries didn't help. In the United States, the Florida and California citrus industries were emerging, decreasing the American demand for Italian lemons and oranges. In addition,

France passed new laws to protect its own vineyards' profits by making it harder for Italian winegrowers to sell their wines in France. That—and an infestation of plant lice in Italy's vineyards—threw thousands of southern Italian winegrowers into financial ruin. All of these changes hit hardest in the south, where most people made their living off of wheat, wine, and fruit.

Not all threats to Italian agriculture came from the outside, however. Deforestation—the cutting down of trees for new farmland—had begun under the Bourbons. Victor Emmanuel's new government accelerated the process, stripping trees from a million acres of land acquired from the Vatican during unification. Without trees to hold it in place, topsoil washed down from formerly fertile higher ground to the lowlands, where it created swamps and blocked streams.

With food harder to grow and money to buy it becoming more scarce, malnutrition became common among the poor southerners. Their weakened state left them especially vulnerable to disease. Epidemics ravaged the countryside. Malaria, an often fatal blood infection carried by some mosquitoes, festered in the newly formed swamps and raged through hundreds of southern towns. At Foca, a village in Calabria, parish records showed 319 births in the last half of the nineteenth century and 516 deaths. Most of the survivors were sick with malaria. Between 1884 and 1887, epidemics of cholera, an intestinal disease, also killed fifty-five thousand Italians.

A Dream Turned to Nightmare

With food production down, many peasants lost their jobs in agriculture. Even *contadini*

A House Made of Stone

Ralph DeRicci, eighty-seven, was the first surviving child of immigrants Rose and John DeRiggi to be born in America. (School officials in Pennsylvania unwittingly changed the spelling of his surname.) In a series of interviews, he described his parents' home in postunification Italy and the difficult lives they led there:

> My parents, they built their house all by themselves. That was in Cicciano, up in the mountains near Naples. My mother, she was tough. The house was made of stone, and she carried all the rocks herself. . . . They used to take a cloth and they'd fold it up to make a pad, and put it on their heads. And then they had a big basket, and they would carry the rocks in it, on their heads.

The DeRiggis owned their home and a small plot of land in Italy, which made them wealthier than many peasants, but they were still poor, said their son, with only enough farmland to eke out a living. "It was very hard. . . . In those days there was no factories or anything like that where you could work. So you had to work on a farm. But if you worked on a farm you hardly could make a living, right? My parents had a field where they used to plant. That's what they made a living out of. But it was hard."

who owned small plots of land had to seek work as laborers in order to feed their families; this resulted in a glut of people looking for jobs. In some places, peasants protested against the government or the landowners, but it had no effect. Italy had too many laborers. Workers who complained or asked for higher wages were simply fired.

The dream of reunification had become a nightmare. Garibaldi had fanned the peasants' desire for freedom. Now they chafed under the control of the north. They were tired of living in crushing poverty, tired of wrestling a living from harsh terrain. For many, the choice was clear. Their hopes for a better life lay across the Atlantic.

CHAPTER TWO

The Decision to Leave

By the 1880s, unemployment, poverty, and desperation had reached critical levels in the Mezzogiorno. The *contadini* had suffered all they could stand. At the same time, one advantage risorgimento had provided them was increased communication between cities and villages. Suddenly the peasants began hearing news of the outside world. Jobs were to be found across the Atlantic, and at wages higher than anything the southern Italians had ever imagined.

At first, only a few hopeful southerners seized the opportunity to create a better life for themselves. Some of the first to go were young men looking to escape Italy's new military draft, instituted by Victor Emmanuel af-

ter unification. Many who stayed and fulfilled their required military service chose to emigrate after their military discharges. In the army, they had become accustomed to abundant food and modern living conditions. So when they returned to their villages, they discovered they no longer had the stomach to live in poverty. Many of them escaped that poverty by sailing for America, and their stories encouraged their neighbors and relatives to do the same.

In 1870, one government official had warned that southern and northern Italians were emigrating in increasing numbers. "Do not delude yourself into thinking that these people are leaving in search of riches," he told his fellow politicians. "They are leaving in tears, cursing the government and the *signori* (wealthy landowners)."[11] Of course some of the immigrants, mostly those who weren't so poor, really were searching for riches, or even adventure. But most, as the official claimed, were fleeing the crushing poverty of the south. They weren't looking to get rich, just to be able to feed their families and escape the control of an uncaring national government and their own tyrannical landowners and overseers.

In his book *The Children of Columbus,* Erik Amfitheatrof summarizes the reasons for southern Italian emigration: "It was the pressure of these many forces, extending deep into history—the ruin of the land, disease, hunger, poverty, but above all the powerless-

ness and the continuation of intolerable social injustice in an age that was bright and promising elsewhere—that caused so many southern Italians to become emigrants."[12] Other observers and many immigrants themselves summed up the reasons in one word: hunger.

The Changing Tides of Immigration

Small numbers of people had been emigrating from Italy for centuries. By 1880, just before the period of mass immigration, almost 118,000 Italians each year left in search of better opportunities. Only 44,000 Italians lived in the United States at that time, almost a quarter of them in New York City. Other Italians had settled in other European countries or in

A Fine Place, Indeed

It wasn't only the poor who felt the lure of a higher standard of living. Even within the much smaller class of merchants and skilled artisans, some southern Italians felt drawn to the greater wealth and opportunity that they believed lay waiting for them across the Atlantic.

Giuseppi Freda was one such dreamer. As a middle-class youngster in Naples, Freda looked ahead to a future full of options. While working in his father's successful ceramics factory, he learned to manufacture utilitarian pieces and delicate decorative objects, and he learned how difficult they could be to sell. He also loved science, and his mother dreamed of his becoming a doctor.

Naples was a major emigration port. As Freda watched ships set sail for America, at first he wondered what would make Italians want to leave their beautiful homeland. Then, one day at the family business, he saw an American buyer purchase a thousand vases for $4,000. The magnitude of the sale astonished the boy. A country whose businessmen could afford such enormous purchases of luxury items, he reasoned, must be a fine place, indeed. And he made up his mind that someday, he, too, would set sail for the United States. Later, medical degree in hand, Freda arrived in New York City, where the size of his first paycheck confirmed his conviction that he had made the right decision in leaving Italy.

South America. Before 1880, 85 percent of Italians who left their country were from the north. Most were educated northerners with specialized skills; until unification, they had more freedom to travel than southerners did. They also had higher literacy levels than southerners and experience in professions besides agriculture, which gave them better prospects of finding jobs elsewhere. However, northerners had fewer reasons to leave their homeland. So for decades, emigration from Italy remained a slow but steady trickle.

The ousting of the Bourbon rulers during the 1860s led to the lifting of travel restrictions that had kept southern peasants in their villages. At first, the leaders of the new Italian government thought this change would make little difference in the south. Italy's rulers saw the southern peasants as a passive people, tied to their ancestral lands and their agricultural tradition. They were wrong. Centuries of surviving earthquakes, rock slides, volcanic eruptions, political turmoil, and the uncertainties of farming had taught the people of the Mezzogiorno to change and adapt. As always, southerners would do what was necessary to survive. And for many, it seemed that the best chance for survival lay outside of Italy, no matter how difficult or frightening the prospect might be.

"Those immigrants had guts," says history professor Michael D'Innocenzo. "It took guts to cross the ocean, you know, for people who had never been out of their village." Such a move defied an ingrained tradition of Italian village life, a mind-set D'Innocenzo calls "the spirit of *campanilismo*," which dictated: "You can only go as far as you can hear the village bell."[13] Leaving the village of one's ancestors took courage—and, sometimes, desperation. Above all, it took hope.

Help Wanted

The possibility of employment was the reason so many Italians were willing to make the trip. Jobs were plentiful in America because of the industrial revolution that was in full swing there. Since the middle of the nineteenth century, the United States and some South American countries had catapulted themselves from agricultural economies to industrial ones. The new factories, railroads, and mines needed huge numbers of unskilled laborers, and there weren't enough of these laborers to keep up with the demand. Unlike Italy, with its glut of workers, America seemed to have jobs for anyone who was willing to start at the bottom and work hard.

In short, American industry was starved for labor. And southern Italy—filled with hungry, poverty-stricken, frustrated people who were accustomed to hard work and desperate for a better life—seemed like a perfect source. To recruit the workers they so badly needed, American companies began sending agents to Italy, where they would travel from village to village, telling stories of wealth and opportunity across the ocean. The companies would offer to pay full or partial travel expenses to able-bodied workers, usually men, who would sign on for jobs in America. Often, those expenses were deducted later from their pay. Such offers were irresistible to peasants who had wanted to leave but hadn't been able to afford the trip. Suddenly they had the means to go. Other peasants were recruited by the steamship companies; their representatives scoured the countryside, look-

Many Italians found work on American railroad lines.

ing for people they could persuade to migrate, thus increasing the number of passengers on their ships.

Word of Mouth

In Italy, close-knit families and villages helped spread emigration fever. It began with the men who left to find work in the United States. In fact, more than half of the first wave of workers to leave Italy for America planned to be gone for only a few months or a few years. They wanted to earn enough money to help their families and then return home. Compared to those in the Mezzogiorno and even northern Italy, wages in America were astronomical. Living conditions were also better, especially for those who were used to rural Italy. In the United States, food was abundant and relatively cheap. For example, in 1880 the average Italian could afford to eat only 28 pounds of meat each year; in the United States, the figure was 120 pounds. And in America, even the working poor could afford wonders such as indoor plumbing, nearly unknown in the villages of southern Italy.

The availability of indoor plumbing and an abundance of food made the standard of living in America much better than that in rural Italy.

As the men saved money and learned to enjoy the higher standard of living in the United States, many changed their minds about returning to Italy. They decided to remain in America permanently. "I came to this country to make a fortune and return to settle in the old country," says one immigrant. "But I changed my mind when I saw that the great thing about this country is that it is good for the working man."[14]

Most of the new immigrants found that life was, indeed, better in the United States. They worked hard, mostly in jobs that required no specialized skills—jobs that few native-born Americans wanted. But the Italians earned more money than they'd ever imagined back home. Just as important, in their adopted homeland, the Italians sensed something they had never felt in Italy: hope. Finally, they had the chance to give their families a better life.

Gradually, news of success in America leaked back across the ocean. As word spread through the cities and villages of southern Italy, the recent immigrants' relatives and neighbors began packing up their own belongings. And the trickle of immigrants swelled to a flood.

"Birds of Passage"

When unskilled Italian men arrived in America, many of them found work that was seasonal; in other words, it was outdoor labor that could be done only during the warmer months of the year. Those who worked for railroads or construction companies, for example, often found themselves out of work in the winter, especially in the cold climate of the northeastern United States. Thus, in the off-season, many men returned to Italy for a few weeks or months. Other workers simply chose to leave their U.S. jobs periodically to return to Italy to visit with their wives or see friends and relatives. Because of their cyclical migrations, those who crossed the ocean repeatedly in this manner became known as "birds of passage."

During return visits to Italy, the birds of passage conspicuously spent U.S. money and bragged about their better lives abroad. Their newly acquired American clothes and goods made them the envy of their former neighbors. Men in the villages wanted to be like them. Women wanted to marry them. Eventually, most of the recent immigrants were able to bring wives and children back to America with them. And many of them, during visits, also enticed their friends and extended families to join them.

Noticing the men's effectiveness as recruiters, U.S. companies began using some of them as labor recruiters in Italy. The birds of passage knew the people and the language. And their families and friends were more likely to trust their word, the word of a fellow villager who told them life was better in America, than that of an American representative. The companies paid the birds of pas-

sage a commission for each new worker they recruited.

John DeRiggi was a bird of passage. According to his American-born son, Ralph DeRicci (the spelling of the surname was inadvertently changed by American school officials), John made seven trips across the Atlantic, beginning in December 1901, before his wife and children were finally able to join him in 1909. In America, DeRiggi worked in northeastern Pennsylvania, laying rails for the Delaware Lackawanna & Western Railroad. His starting wage there was thirty-two cents an hour, more than ten times what he could make in Italy; eventually, his pay was raised to forty cents an hour.

"In the summertime . . . ," says DeRicci, "he would get a job and work on the railroad. And then in the wintertime when the weather was real bad, there wouldn't be too much work, you know, and so he would save

Men who worked seasonally in the United States became known as "birds of passage."

enough money and then he would go back to Europe. And he would stay there maybe a month or two, and then he would go back to Pennsylvania." For the first few years, De-Ricci's mother, Rose, and his older brothers and sisters remained in Cicciano, a hill town outside of Naples. "He didn't bring her [his wife] here [to America] 'til quite a while later. That's why he made so many trips."[15]

Children of the "birds of passage," like John DeRiggi's oldest son, Joe, often waited years before following their fathers to America.

Efforts to Halt Immigration

During the 1870s and 1880s, immigration was just beginning to pick up speed, but some Italian officials already worried that the flow of people out of the country would leave Italy's industries—and eventually, even its orchards, fields, and vineyards—without enough workers. Thus, some members of Italy's legislative body, the Chamber of Deputies, proposed a controversial new law to prevent emigration. Others blocked the law, arguing that it would impinge on citizens' rights. Deprived of a legislative solution, opponents of immigration turned to other methods of keeping Italians in Italy. For instance, in northern Italy's Lombardy, one of the nation's most prosperous agricultural regions, authorities attempted to delay the passports of a group of workers trying to leave the country. The workers retaliated by setting fire to dairy farms, yelling, "To America! To America!"

Other immigration opponents tried to frighten Italians into staying. Anti-immigration factions in the Chamber of Deputies and among the right-wing elements of the Catholic Church produced false letters, supposedly from Italians living in the United States and South America. In these letters, alleged immigrants recounted the horrors of their lives abroad. Instead of a higher standard of living, they claimed to have found only hunger and disease. They told of imprisonment and near slavery in forced labor camps, and warned of unscrupulous labor recruiters and steamship agents.

Such scare tactics failed, however. From the villages of Sicily to the cities of northern Italy, people saw the fine clothes and American dollars of their returning friends and rel-

Most immigrants were not swayed by the Italian government's false advertisements of life in America.

atives. And despite the words of unscrupulous politicians, they continued to believe in the promise of a better life across the ocean.

Intermediate Stops

Some Italians immigrated to the United States by way of other countries. This was especially true of Italians from regions north of Rome, because of the relatively short distances between northern Italy and other European countries. A relocation to a European country such as nearby France or Switzerland, or to a North African nation, was quicker and less daunting than a long sea voyage. Some of these immigrants took temporary jobs in mining or in the building trades there in order to supplement their incomes

and then returned home. Other families moved there for indefinite periods of time, hoping the change would allow them to improve their lives while still remaining close enough to visit friends and relatives—and to return home if things didn't work out. Eventually, many of these people immigrated to America, though, where jobs were more plentiful and higher paying.

Mary Ciabocchi, who was born Maria Piccioli in 1913, tells one such story. Her parents lived in Serravalle, in central Italy, where they farmed for a living. "They had a big garden, because what kind of work did they have there? They didn't have coal mines. They didn't have factories." She says her parents left Serravalle for France when her mother found a job there as a wet nurse.

Francesca Piccioli (left) and her daughter Pierina (right) lived in France for two years before joining Francesca's husband in Pennsylvania.

"A rich lady there had a baby, and she [the lady] couldn't nurse, so she hired my mother to nurse her baby. That was in France."[16]

Fortunato and Francesca Piccioli, Mary's parents, moved to France with their sons. Their first daughter, Pierina, was born there in January 1907. Fortunato immigrated to America in November of that year to find a job and prepare for his family's eventual arrival. After two years, the French woman's

baby was weaned. Once Francesca's position as a wet nurse ended, she and her three children—ages ten, six, and two—traveled to the port of Le Havre, France, where they boarded a steamship called the *Chicago*. They arrived at Ellis Island on April 27, 1909, and joined Fortunato in Peckville, Pennsylvania.

Changing Social Customs

Though many native-born U.S. residents welcomed the Italian men as laborers, few wanted them to marry into their families. Furthermore, the language barrier and the Italians' own social customs dictated that Italian men, even those with jobs in the United States, marry women from home. So, single men often returned to Italy to find wives. Sometimes this was difficult. According to Italian tradition, not just the couple but their parents had to agree on a match. At times, a woman's parents balked at allowing their daughter to marry one of the birds of passage, afraid she would travel to America with him and the family would never see her again. Some women had similar reactions, preferring to remain in familiar surroundings.

Many women, though, were excited by the possibilities the birds of passage offered. The men's visits changed the women and their villages forever, setting the scene for yet more emigration. Gay Talese describes the effects the men's visits home had on his father's village, Maida, and especially on the young women there. He says that even if a woman chose to stay at home after getting to know the visitors from America, "the typical village maiden was no longer contented with what she had—her horizons had been widened, options were in the offing; the hometown *boule-*

vardiers [townspeople taking an evening stroll], walking in circles, now lacked the mystery of the men visiting from abroad."[17]

These evening walks along the boulevards and through the town's center plaza were a common social activity in Maida and other Italian villages. This was a time to catch up on gossip, greet friends, and observe neighbors. But strict customs were observed during the nightly promenade. Men strolled arm in arm, their choice of companions determined by rank, occupation, and status in the community. Mothers walked with their daughters of marriageable age. A man would never catch the eye of an unchaperoned woman; even a glance could damage both their reputations. This evening stroll reinforced class structures in the villages—until the visiting birds of passage arrived and began ignoring the protocols.

According to Talese, their time abroad and their newfound wealth desensitized some of

White Widows

In many families, wives and children stayed in Italy, at least for a time, after their husbands and fathers immigrated to America. These women's lives were lonely. But at the same time, many of these women, called "white widows," found a new kind of freedom in their solitude, bolstered by an influx of cash from their distant husbands.

Especially in the rural villages of the south, customs and attitudes strictly confined a woman's role. An unmarried woman was expected to defer to her father's wishes; a married woman, to her husband's. In some ways, a white widow had the best of both worlds. She enjoyed a married woman's social status and source of income but did not have to submit to her husband's will in making day-to-day decisions.

In other cases, a man left behind a wife or girlfriend in Italy because she refused to leave her family and friends. Some of these men maintained families in both the United States and Italy simultaneously. In a series of interviews, Ralph DeRicci, the eighty-six-year-old son of immigrants, explains this.

"It used to happen a lot. My Uncle Louie DeStefano done that. He must have been on my mother's side. My uncle lived with us in Pennsylvania and my mother used to . . . have a bankbook for him." Every payday, after DeRicci's uncle had paid his mother for room and board, she put money into an account for him to save up enough so that he could eventually send for his wife to join him from Italy. "So then, when she was about ready to come here, my mother gave him the money. He turned around and he sent his wife the money. And when she got the money she took it and she spent it, so she didn't come. So he never bothered with her no more. So then he got married in this country. But he never told his new wife, Emma, that he was already married. When the first wife got that money, she must have thought she was rich."

the young men to the local customs. They began acting superior to their former neighbors, ignoring the protocols that dictated whom they could walk with or speak to. They also became less respectful of their elders and more impatient with the courting rituals that required them to negotiate with a young woman's parents instead of flirting with her directly and going on dates as a couple. Furthermore, the returning immigrants exposed more and more peasants to new American attitudes and customs, which emphasized social equality and greater sexual freedom. In the process, the birds of passage began changing young Italians' ambitions and expectations. This, in turn, enticed other townspeople into leaving Italy.

Italy's economy improved as immigrants imported Italian food products to the United States.

An Influx of Cash

Even when they weren't visiting Italy, the birds of passage managed to remind their fellow villagers of their successes in America. As they mined coal beneath the Pennsylvania hills, hauled nets on New Orleans fishing boats, dug subway tunnels in New York, or carved stone monuments in Washington, D.C., the men saved their wages and sent money back to their families.

In fact, people who left Italy to escape poverty actually helped relieve the country's poverty by dutifully sending some of their earnings home. In 1901, for instance, the average working immigrant contributed $250 in cash to Italian relatives. That was a huge sum at a time when a southern Italian farmworker might earn less than $100 a year. By 1914, immigrants had sent more than $700 million back to Italy, adding greatly to the nation's economy and allowing family members to follow their wage earners westward.

The Italian Americans in the United States also helped Italy's economy by creating a new market for Italian goods. For years, Italian exports had been losing ground as people in other countries bought wine from France and citrus fruits from the United States. But the new immigrants craved the foods and other Italian products of their homeland. That created more demand for Italian-made goods in the United States, helping to boost the sagging Italian agricultural industry.

By the 1890s, there was no stemming the tide of immigration. Italians were leaving Italy in unprecedented numbers. Armed with little more than hope, courage, and the traditions that had sustained them through hardship and deprivation, they turned their backs on poverty and oppression in order to make new lives for themselves and their families.

CHAPTER THREE

Atlantic Crossing

Before they could settle in the United States, immigrants faced a series of daunting challenges. They could not leave Italy until they had successfully wound their way through a series of perplexing administrative procedures and regulations, which were made more complicated by the fact that most of the immigrants were illiterate. Then, they had to endure a long and arduous ocean voyage in order to reach their new country.

Obtaining the Documents

The headaches began at home, where a would-be traveler had to obtain two docu-ments, beginning with a birth certificate from the village secretary. The police headquarters in the provincial capital required the birth cer-tificate before officials would issue the sec-ond document, a *nulla osta,* which verified legal permission to emigrate. Someone who was wanted for a crime in Italy could not legally obtain a *nulla osta;* neither could a man who had been drafted and was trying to avoid reporting for military duty. Navigating the succession of paperwork was confusing and difficult, but nobody could board a ship without the proper documents.

Papers in hand, the hopeful immigrants sold some of their possessions and packed the rest. Then they said good-bye to family and friends and set out for their new lives. It was a time of hope, but for many it was also a time of overwhelming grief as they were leaving everyone and everything familiar. One immigrant describes the night he left his home and family:

> My father . . . put my valises [suitcases] on the old mule, Old Titi, and we went up to the railroad station. It was pitch dark, early in the morning. From the cracks in the shutters over here and over there I could see the yellow light of the oil lamps. The streets were empty. I could smell the air like when the hay is damp. I could hear behind the doors the stamping of a mule, a horse breathing. At another door, somebody snoring. My father did not speak all the way to the train. I don't know when he said it to me, my father, he said, "Make yourself courage." And that was the last time I saw my father."[18]

The First Leg

The first leg of the journey involved traveling to a port. Naples, in southern Italy, was the most popular exit port for overseas travelers. Other ports included Palermo, on the island of Sicily; Messina, also Sicilian but on the strait that separates the island from Calabria on the mainland; and Genoa, in the north. Some Italian immigrants from the north embarked from ports across the border in Austria or France if they happened to live closer to those foreign ports than to Genoa or other Italian ports. Throughout Italy, hopeful immigrants traveled to the port cities on foot, by horse-drawn cart, by donkey, or by railroad.

And they brought with them things they might need in America. "No matter how they traveled," say historians Ben Morreale and Robert Carola, "all these displaced pioneers carried all their possessions with them. (Italians seemed to prefer to take along their bedding and feather mattresses.) Everyone, even the children, carried something. If a mother held a child in each hand she carried a package with her teeth."[19]

Frank Santoni, an immigrant who was born in 1892 in Campofiorito, Sicily, describes the start of his journey and the largest piece of luggage his family carried:

> I remember that we left in a cart, a two-wheeled cart with a big homemade trunk, I would say perhaps five feet wide, three feet deep, and three feet high. It was well made, because it took the whole trip to America, and we had that trunk for many, many years. I think I can remember it being in my family even when I got married, and for twenty-five to thirty years after we got to America.[20]

Waiting to Embark

Some immigrants arrived in Naples or another port city with steamship tickets in hand. They had received them from relatives in the United States or had purchased them in their hometowns as part of a package deal that included their transportation from home all the way to America. Other hopeful immigrants came without having booked their passage ahead of time. These individuals faced the often confusing ordeal of trying to buy tickets in an unfamiliar city, often from dishonest vendors who inflated the price and pocketed the profits.

Because land travel through rural areas was unpredictable, immigrants sometimes had to remain in port for days or weeks while they waited for a slot on an outgoing steamship. The bustling port cities terrified some rural villagers, most of whom had never seen a large city. Other immigrants, especially the young and adventurous, found the cities exhilarating. "The three days in Naples were lovely," said Rosa Martino, who was eighteen years old in 1922 when she and her brother emigrated from Sicily. "On every corner was somebody with a guitar and a mandolin—singing, singing. I thought Naples was the most beautiful city in the world. There were a lot of young boys, young girls, that would come to this country [America]. So you can imagine the really wonderful time that I had."[21]

While they waited in Naples and the other port cities, travelers shared lodgings with other immigrants or slept out in the open. Unscrupulous peddlers, porters, ticket sellers, pickpockets, and other swindlers preyed on the naive and overwhelmed travelers. Some offered to carry the immigrants' belongings onto the ship and then walked away with the bags. Others sold fake cures for trachoma, a contagious eye disease; U.S. immigration officials denied entry to anyone afflicted with the disease. Still other swindlers dressed as priests or monks and peddled pictures of saints, claiming that carrying the icons would ensure safe passage.

Preboarding Screenings

After surviving the attentions of those intent on defrauding them, the travelers faced an

A voyage to America began with traveling to a port city, like Palermo (pictured).

even more intimidating challenge. Beginning in 1891, a U.S. law required shipping firms to screen all passengers for medical conditions before they boarded the ships. So, immigrants had to be disinfected, vaccinated, and checked for obvious signs of illness before they began the journey.

At most ports, though, this screening was cursory, and the United States ended up deporting thousands who arrived with medical conditions that might have been successfully treated in their own country before they left. Such conditions included trachoma, a contagious scalp disease called favus, general physical weakness, and various mental illnesses. Many families who faced this situation were torn apart; one sick family member was sent home while the others settled in America. Most of these men, women, and children had sacrificed everything to make the trip. They returned to Europe destitute, discouraged, and homeless.

Fiorello H. LaGuardia was largely responsible for reforms that drastically reduced the numbers of would-be Italian Americans who were sent back to Italy. The American-born son of Italian immigrants, LaGuardia is best known for his years as mayor of New York City during the mid–twentieth century. But starting at age twenty, he served as an American consul in Fiume, a port city, from 1903 until 1906. Fiume was not actually Italian. It was in Austro-Hungarian territory, near Italy's northeastern border, which made it a major exit port for emigrants from nearby parts of Italy. LaGuardia's work there—and later at Ellis Island, the U.S. entry port for most Italian Americans—opened his eyes to the hardships immigrants endured. He hated seeing Italians deported back to Europe after the United States rejected them for medical reasons. As he later recounted,

Several hundred immigrants daily [at Ellis Island] were found to be suffering from trachoma and their exclusion was mandatory. It was harrowing to see families separated because the precau-

Even though immigrants went through a screening process before leaving Italy, some immigrants were still deported upon reaching the United States because they were deemed too ill to enter the country.

tion had not been taken of giving them prior examinations on the other side. Sometimes, if it was a young child who suffered from trachoma, one of the parents had to return to the native country with the rejected member of the family. When they learned their fate, they were stunned. [22]

From his first day on the job in Fiume, La-Guardia insisted on thorough medical exams rather than the usual cursory screenings for all departing passengers. The shipping companies balked at spending the extra money, but LaGuardia fought them and won. As a result, among shiploads under LaGuardia's jurisdiction, the numbers of rejected immigrants plummeted. By 1908, the Italian government had taken notice and adopted his policies nationwide, and Italy became the only country that didn't routinely have thousands of its immigrants rejected at Ellis Island. Eventually, the United States also instituted LaGuardia's reforms, requiring the immigrants' primary medical examinations to take place before they boarded the ships in their home countries.

The Sea Voyage Begins

After passing the medical screenings, the immigrants were cleared to board the vessels that would carry them to their new home. They booked passage on ships of various sizes and vintages. Large, modern ocean liners moved more swiftly and smoothly through turbulent waters than did the smaller, older models. These newer ships also boasted radio communication technology, pioneered by a young Italian who had also traveled to

Shipboard Fun

For some immigrant children, the Atlantic crossing was the adventure of a lifetime, filled with chances to explore and encounters with new things. Frank Santori was seven years old in 1900 when his family left Sicily for the United States, traveling in steerage. He told his story in *Island of Hope, Island of Tears,* by David M. Brownstone, Irene M. Franck, and Douglass L. Brownstone.

"We [my older brother and I] roamed the ship and a very funny thing was we came near the kitchen and we saw the goodies going on there." The kitchen had an ice cream freezer for providing confections to the first- and second-class passengers. At the time, ice cream was homemade, using ice and salt along with the cream mixture. "We took the covers from the containers. . . . Lo and behold, we saw the ice and salt—and we saw something there that we didn't know. We didn't even taste it, for some reason or another. We did know the ice. We quickly got hold of a nice piece of ice, closed the thing, and went about our business, not knowing what ice cream was."

America, Guglielmo Marconi. Steamships were the norm, but some immigrants traveled on ships powered by sails. Not all of the ships were Italian owned; many ships that sailed from Italian ports hailed from countries throughout Europe.

A sea voyage to America could be both frightening and fun for the immigrants.

During the peak immigration years, ships left frequently for the United States, and most immigrants waited in the port cities for less than two weeks. As passengers finally arrived at their ships and began to board, the general mood was a combination of confusion, excitement, and nervous tension. Edmondo De Amicis, who sailed from Genoa to the United States in 1890, described the crowd that boarded the *Galileo,* the ship on which he traveled:

> Workmen, peasants, women with children at the breast, little fellows with the tin medal of the infant asylum still hanging around their necks passed on their way, and almost everyone was carrying something. They had folding chairs, they had bags and trunks of every shape in their hands or on their heads; their arms were full of mattresses and bedclothes, and their . . . tickets were held fast in their mouths. . . . Old peasant women in wooden shoes, holding up their skirts so as not to stumble over the cleats of the gangplank, showed bare legs that were like sticks. Many were barefoot and had their shoes hung around their necks. . . . At last, sailors were heard shouting fore and aft, *"Chi non et passeggero, a terra"*—"All ashore that's going ashore." These words sent a thrill from one end of the *Galileo* to the other. In a few moments all strangers were out of the ship, the bridge was hauled ashore . . . the entering port closed, a whistle sounded, and the ship began to move. Then women burst out crying, youths who had been laughing grew serious, and bearded men hitherto stolid were seen to pass a hand across the eyes.[23]

Traveling Steerage: Human Cargo

Three classes of passengers boarded the ships. Whether first-class, second-class, or third-class, a typical traveler knew little of the existence of the other classes. Areas of the ship were strictly divided to keep them apart. In particular, first- and second-class passengers seldom saw any sign that hundreds of indigent people shared their voyage, huddled in misery just a few decks beneath them.

Nearly all immigrants traveled in third class, known as "steerage" because the accommodations were near the ship's steering mechanism and engines. Because of the horrors of steerage travel, many immigrants dubbed the ocean crossing the *via dolorosa,* or "sorrowful way." Passengers in steerage were treated much like cargo. They endured primitive and cramped conditions deep in the bowels of the ship, with no privacy, no ventilation, and poor food. Ceilings could be as low as six feet; corridors were dark and narrow. A typical steamship line crammed between three hundred and six hundred people into a steerage section, and some of the huge luxury liners packed in many more. Men were separated from women and children, sometimes in different compartments and other times with partitions made of sheets hung over ropes. People slept in narrow triple-decker bunks that might or might not have mattresses provided.

Francesco Ventrasca, who sailed in steerage from Naples on the French liner *Champagne,* later wrote about the Atlantic crossing:

There were over a thousand of us on board. I recall only steerage. I did not venture to speculate on higher living. Most of us were assigned to bunks— berths would be too refined a name for them. Some of the men were placed one story below the deck and others two stories below. We managed to get a bit of light through the hatchway or through the portholes. No one could stay below for very long [because of the smell]. We were all the time on deck, except at night and in stormy weather—and we had plenty of that.[24]

Years later, many immigrants could still describe the smells of the steerage section.

As immigrants boarded ships bound for America, they were both excited and nervous.

The travelers used oil lamps for light, and the odor of the oil mingled with the aromas of urine, vomit, the ship's engines, livestock being shipped to America, and the barrels of herring that, on many ships, provided the immigrants' only food beyond what they brought themselves. (The shipping companies served herring because the fish cost very little and kept passengers reasonably healthy for the duration of the passage.)

A Funny Thing Happened on the Way to Ellis Island

In an interview with the author, Ralph DeRicci tells of a near disaster that took place during one of the trips his father, John DeRiggi, took, traveling from Naples to New York in the years before the rest of his family immigrated.

My father made seven trips, you know, back and forth. They were sailing ships, but I guess they must have had some kind of steam power. . . . In them days the ships used to have steam and sails, you know. . . . But this one time when he went, the ship broke down and they couldn't fix it.

They were in deep water and you couldn't drop an anchor because it was too deep. So they just drifted. And they drifted all night long, and then there was an island there. And they drifted by this island.

And the captain figured that, you know, the water wasn't that deep, so . . . they dropped anchor there. They stayed on the ship but they couldn't fix it; they didn't have no parts. So then they decided to send some of the men to this island to see if there was anything there that they could eat, because they had finished eating everything they had on the ship. The men went in a rowboat. They went to shore and they found different kinds of fruit and stuff. They got so that they took some of the women to the island too, you know. At nighttime they would go back to the ship to sleep. And then in the daytime they would go to this island. And they were there for a couple of weeks.

Then they woke up one morning and there was another ship broke down, and I guess the way the currents worked they had took it to the same place. And between the first ship that was broke, and this new one here that had broken, they were able to salvage enough parts to get one going. So then what they done, they took all the women and children and put them on that other ship that they got fixed. And then they come back to America and they sent somebody back for the men later on, you know, to help to get them. That's how they got off the island.

But my mother back in Italy, she thought my father was dead, like the boat had sunk, when nobody heard nothing from them. And then she found out he was alive.

The trip usually took about two weeks, but depending on the type of ship and the weather conditions, it could last as little as a week or as long as a month. Fresh water was available only on deck. Toilets were inconveniently located, and were sometimes no more than drains in the floor.

Because of the smells and the poor food—and because people on the lower decks of the ship suffered the most from the pounding of the engines and the waves—steerage passengers were especially prone to seasickness. Rocco Corresca and his brother Francesco, for example, were orphans who grew up on the streets of Naples. The boys earned their passage by working in the boiler room of a ship bound for the United States. There, they were plagued by seasickness, made worse by the heat of the fires.

"We had to carry coal to the place where it could be thrown on the fires," Corresca remembers. "Francesco and I were very sick . . . and lay on the coal for a long time, but they threw water on us and made us get up. We could not stand on our feet well, for everything was going around and we had no strength. We said that we wished we had stayed in Italy no matter how much gold there was in America. We could not eat for three days."[25]

Almost all the immigrants who came to America during the Ellis Island period traveled steerage. They tolerated its horrors because steerage was cheap. Before World War I, steerage fare across the Atlantic usually cost between $15 and $25 per person. Even during and after the war, when fares rose, it was

Many immigrants felt that the opportunities America offered would be worth enduring the Atlantic crossing.

still by far the least expensive way to cross the ocean.

Via Dolorosa

Ocean travel at the time could be hazardous, especially in older vessels. Some immigrant ships broke down or met with accidents on the tumultuous seas. Some actually capsized; others experienced outbreaks of contagious diseases. But despite the risks and the horrors of the *via dolorosa,* millions of Italians clamored to make the trip.

The peasants of the Mezzogiorno were used to hardship and poor treatment; generations of desperate poverty, political oppression, and backbreaking labor had acclimated them to suffering. They told themselves that the chance at a new life in the United States was worth whatever they might have to endure aboard the ship. And as they stood at the ship's railing, gazing westward across the waves, they dreamed of open spaces, plentiful food, and welcoming communities.

CHAPTER FOUR

Welcome to America

The first sight of America from the deck of a ship mesmerized most immigrants. Others felt only a numb relief at the end of the long and wretched journey. A cry would echo out, *"Lamerica! lamerica!"* and people would crowd one side of the deck to see New York Harbor and the still-new Statue of Liberty, erected in 1886.

Author Gay Talese's father, Joseph, remembered the cold December dawn in 1920 when his ship sailed into the harbor. Fog shrouded the Statue of Liberty, hiding it from view, but the waters were calm—a welcome relief to the seasick-prone teenager. Dressed in his best suit, as well as an overcoat and other winter weather gear, he stood on the deck and watched as his new country drew near. Joseph, who had spent much of the trip seasick in his second-class cabin, had enjoyed little contact with the other passengers. The ship had left from France instead of his native Italy; thus, most people on the second-class deck that day were from other European countries, with different climates, clothing, and customs than what he was used to. In addition, many of the second-class passengers were Americans returning home. The diverse mix of people overwhelmed the teenager.

"Despite his clothes he was extremely cold," Gay Talese says of his father, Joseph, "and he huddled close to the people standing three deep along the rail."

Many of the women, and even a few men, wore full-length fur coats. Joseph had never before seen men in fur, nor had he ever seen men drinking from flasks, as several were now doing. Some of the young women, their bobbed heads covered with turbans or small-brimmed hats, also drank from the silver containers that the men passed around. What most surprised him was the carefree manner in which the women put to their lips what seconds before had touched the lips of several men. Joseph was indeed entering the New World. . . . [The passengers on deck applauded] as the sun streamed through the clouds and the skyline of lower Manhattan came vaguely into view. At first glance Joseph thought he was sailing toward a cluster of cornstalks, dense and golden in the misty morning light.[26]

Immigrants aboard a ship wave and cheer as New York's Statue of Liberty comes into view.

Arriving ships docked first at a Manhattan pier. There, immigration officials quickly processed first- and second-class passengers so they could get on with their new lives. Steerage passengers, on the other hand, lined up to board a ferry or barge to Ellis Island, where they faced yet another confusing and dehumanizing ordeal.

A First Taste of America

Immigrants arriving at Ellis Island looked forward to long waits, long lines, and compli-cated instructions. At best, the processing took hours. In worse cases, hopeful immigrants were detained for days; some were even sent back to Italy.

Not all the news was bad. Aboard the ships, many of the travelers had subsisted for weeks on little more than herring. Now they were greeted with food that, while sometimes unfamiliar, was served in amounts that astonished the malnourished peasants from the Mezzogiorno. For many, it confirmed their dreams of America as a land of plenty. Young immigrant Frank Santoni describes a snack he

Ellis Island: America's Gateway

Until 1892, most arriving Italian immigrants were processed at Castle Garden, a facility on the tip of Manhattan. When the numbers of Italian and other immigrants skyrocketed during the last decades of the nineteenth century, Castle Garden proved too small and inefficient for the task. Besides, its Manhattan location made it too easily accessible for swindlers who sought to take advantage of the frightened, disoriented travelers. To take control of the situation, the U.S. government decided to isolate new arrivals as soon as they disembarked. The solution was a new processing center on Ellis Island, in upper New York Bay near the New Jersey shore.

From its opening in 1892, Ellis Island was the main port of entry for almost all Italian arrivals, even as work continued on its construction. Five years after its inauguration—and the day after the final phase of construction was completed—a fire gutted all of the buildings, which had been made of wood. A newly rebuilt Ellis Island opened in 1900, boasting the distinctive brick structures that still greet visitors today. In addition to wharves and the main processing center, Ellis Island's facilities included dormitories, medical centers, a restaurant, laundry facilities, a bathhouse, and a playground.

Between 1900 and 1910, almost 9 million immigrants passed through Ellis Island, more than 2 million of them from Italy. The sheer volume of immigrants gradually overwhelmed even the new and improved facilities, necessitating further expansion.

Ellis Island operated as an immigration processing center until 1954. During its sixty-two years of operation, the island was the site of 355 births and more than 3,500 deaths. In 1992 the abandoned, dilapidated structures were restored and opened to the public as a museum of immigration.

Free, hot meals were served to immigrants who were detained on Ellis Island for more than a few hours.

received from an Italian social service organization as he waited in line to be examined: "As we got off the boat at Ellis Island we were given bread, which I relished very much, Italian bread, about twelve inches long, intermingled, twisted. I enjoyed it. And we were given wine, even at that age [seven], we were given wine to drink. . . . It was a very heavy wine. It was pretty muddy. I didn't like it. I didn't drink very much. I liked the bread."[27]

Along with snacks for arriving immigrants, workers prepared boxed meals that immigrants could buy for a dollar to take with them when they were released. In some cases, relief organizations bought the boxed meals for them. Helen Barth, an Ellis Island social worker, remembers those boxed lunches with mixed feelings:

I never could stand the odor when I went near those kitchens. It was awful. A lot of food. The food was all right . . . but the place wasn't clean, and the odors were just awful. . . . In those boxes, if they were Jewish immigrants, they would get cheese sandwiches. If they were Christian immigrants, they would get ham. And they were very happy and thankful for a can of sardines and bread. They were very happy and thankful to get those boxes.

But I was sick when I saw those boxes, because we had a dining room where people came from outside to make those sandwiches. The food was spread out on the table with cheese and big mounds of ham and when the four o'clock whistle blew, everybody stopped working. They didn't clear the tables and put the food back in the icebox where it belonged, but left it on the tables. . . . We had so many rats there, on Ellis Island. If you took a walk on the boardwalk, you could see them playing on the piers. It was really awful. But nobody seemed to mind. In fact, if someone was eating a sandwich, it would be nothing to throw a piece of it down to feed the rats."[28]

Immigrants who had to stay at Ellis Island more than a few hours were served free hot meals during their time there. At a typical luncheon in 1906, for instance, they ate beef stew, boiled potatoes, and rye bread. In the immigrant dining halls, people sat tightly crowded at long tables.

Abuse and Reform

A full stomach made many immigrants feel better, but food couldn't do much to ease the trials ahead. Early in the history of Ellis Island, reports of corruption were rampant. The average family arrived with less than $20, but unscrupulous immigration employees tried to steal as much of it as they could. Some employees cheated the immigrants when exchanging their currency into dollars. Some offered to speed people through the process in return for cash. Others tried to sell the newcomers forged citizenship documents that would allow them to bypass the examinations and proceed directly to the mainland.

Reports of such abuses are hard to come by from the immigrants themselves because few had any way of knowing they were being exploited. But one minister, Edward Steiner, conducted experiments to see if rumors of abuses were true. To find out, he himself traveled in steerage several times in order to experience the same conditions the immigrants faced. "I knew that the money changers were 'crooked,'" he wrote afterward, "so I passed a 20 mark piece to one of them for exchange, and was cheated out of nearly 75 percent of my money. My change was largely composed of new pennies, whose brightness was well calculated to deceive any newcomer."[29]

When Theodore Roosevelt became president in 1901, he took steps to clean up the abuses. He fired the corrupt officials who had been overseeing operations on the island and replaced them with people who had reputations for honesty and efficiency, including William Williams, his new, handpicked commissioner for Ellis Island. After taking over in 1902, Williams's first act in office was to let employees know that anyone who cheated the immigrants would be out of a job. Furthermore, he terminated the contracts of dishonest companies that had been hired to prepare food for the immigrants, handle their baggage, and exchange their money.

Williams was not perfect, however. He considered people from southern and eastern Europe to be "low-grade immigrants" and made no secret of his preference for northern Europeans. In 1904 he even instituted a policy, unsupported by the existing immigration laws, that required immigrants to show that they had $10 per person, as well as tickets to reach their final destination, before they could be approved for entrance. In 1909 he increased the amount to $25 per person. The regulation was applied inconsistently, most often against southern and eastern Europeans, which included Italians. Despite his sometimes unfair policies, Williams did improve conditions for the entering immigrants. Under his rule, workers at Ellis Island were strictly prohibited from profiting personally through exploiting the newcomers.

President Roosevelt kept a careful eye on the island to be sure that reforms were being made. In 1903, during a surprise visit to the island, he personally liberated a woman and four children who had been held there for nearly two months awaiting a decision on their immigration status. As a result of Roosevelt's concern and Williams's management, within a few years, arriving immigrants navigated a processing system at Ellis Island that was basically honest, though still perplexing and traumatic.

The Processing Begins

The wharves at Ellis Island were large enough to receive two shiploads of people simultaneously. Immigrants lined up and proceeded into the main building. First, they entered the enormous Great Hall, a room that measured two hundred feet by one hundred feet with a soaring fifty-six-foot ceiling. After two weeks in a ship's cramped steerage compartments, the room must have seemed as spacious as the sky. In the Great Hall, the newcomers were told to leave their bags in storage. Most feared they would never see their meager possessions again.

Then it was time to embark on an inspection process that was harrowing for most immigrants. In general, the immigrants spoke little English and had no idea what was happening or what to expect.

Immigrants wait in Ellis Island's Great Hall to be processed for entrance into the United States.

Mystifying and sometimes painful medical tests, a bewildering series of lines to stand in and people to be approved by, and barely understood questions about their health, background, and prospects left many terrified. Anyone who was suspect for physical, mental, or financial reasons could be detained at the island for hours, days, weeks, or even months, often with little explanation. The least fortunate ones were rejected and sent back home. Because of the fear and uncertainty, Italian immigrants who had been through Ellis Island called it *isola della lacrime,* or "island of tears."

The authors of *Island of Hope, Island of Tears* describe the scene that greeted the new arrivals as they lined up for processing:

> Many of those coming through Ellis Island had very little trouble themselves, yet saw the place as truly an "island of tears," of bars, cages and callous brutality. They saw iron railings covering most of the floor of the Great Hall. The bars were there to create aisles for orderly movement . . . they saw them as the iron bars of a prison. They saw wired detention areas, which they identified as cages. They saw people detained, heard people crying. . . . The crying epidemic there started the day it opened, was fed by exhaustion, fear, confusion, and tragedy . . . and by the Island's personnel. Many were no worse than bureaucrats everywhere, some a great deal better than they had any reason to be, themselves exhausted by the enormous and never-ending workload under conditions of extreme crowding and tension—and by the crying that never stopped.[30]

Immigrants were given numbered tags to identify them for their medical examinations.

Medical Examinations

First, officials pinned a large white tag to each person's clothing that contained the name of the vessel he or she had arrived on, the immigrant's name, and a letter and number used for identification. Then employees herded the immigrants up a long flight of stairs to the medical inspection center, which until 1911 was on the building's second floor. (In later years, medical personnel conducted the examinations in first-floor facilities.)

As the immigrants climbed the steps, doctors observed them closely for signs of physical weakness and scrawled coded chalk marks on the backs of any who appeared sick or disabled. For example, a "C" on an immigrant's coat meant doctors suspected conjunctivitis, an eye infection also known as pinkeye. "Ct" meant trachoma, another eye disease that caused many arrivals to be rejected. "H" stood for heart problems. "L" stood for lameness. "S" meant senility.

Once the immigrants reached the examination area, doctors examined men and women in separate rooms, forcing families to split up for hours, sometimes with children temporarily taken from their parents. The exams covered a wide variety of mental and physical impairments. Again, anyone suspected of being ill was marked with chalk and detained for further screening. Up to half of all arriving passengers received chalk marks and had to endure special scrutiny.

The standard medical inspection had two parts. For someone in good health, the primary medical exam took no more than two minutes. For those who were thought to be ill, it could take much longer.

The next exam was for trachoma and other eye problems. This painful and terrifying procedure involved turning an immigrant's

Inspectors use buttonhooks to test immigrants for eye disease.

eyelids inside out, using a buttonhook. Some newcomers were incorrectly diagnosed with the disease because their eyes were red from crying. After medical personnel had finished prodding and observing, the immigrants moved back to the Great Hall for the next stage of processing.

Questions and Answers

In the Great Hall, a maze of aisles separated by iron railings helped guide the new arrivals to the proper places. They were arranged alphabetically by name and by country of ori-

Cagelike detention areas frightened immigrants awaiting interrogation.

gin. This system bewildered the Italians, who for the most part could not read and were not used to crowds. In full view were the temporary detention areas for those whose fitness to enter the country was in question, people who, officials suspected, among other things, might be ill, have criminal backgrounds, or be likely to end up as prostitutes or wards of the state. These wire-enclosed detention areas frightened the other immigrants, who thought they resembled cages and feared being placed there.

The newcomers waited in line in the Great Hall until they could speak through interpreters to a clerk and answer a list of questions. Among other things, the clerks needed to know each immigrant's full name, to check it against a ship's manifest; last place of residence; literacy skills; final destination; funding source for the voyage; and amount of cash on hand.

Even the seemingly simple question "What is your name?" could cause confusion, resulting in many Italians settling into their new homes with different names than the ones with which they left Italy. Some renamed themselves to sound more American; for example, Rossi might become Ross. Others created new names to hide from the Italian draft or because they were wanted by authorities for demonstrating against the Italian government.

Most name changes, however, were probably simple misunderstandings. Immigration clerks read passenger names off of handwritten ships' manifests. Shipping line employees had made those lists during rushed preboarding interviews. Those interviews and the ones at Ellis Island both provided opportunities for mistakes. The handwriting might be illegible.

"What If They Send Me Back to Italy?"

Rita Alfano, a Sicilian widow, arrived at Ellis Island in 1905 with her five-year-old daughter, Fortunata. The pair breezed through the medical exams, but Alfano's sister-in-law, who lived in Rochester, New York, arrived to pick up the pair alone, without her husband. Unwilling to release them into the custody of an unaccompanied woman, authorities detained Alfano and her daughter.

As the days passed, Alfano became more and more desperate. Her late husband's family back in Sicily had refused to support her any longer; if she were forced to return to Italy, she might be forced into prostitution or a convent in order to survive. Either way, she would have to give up her child to an orphanage.

"On the third day of her [Alfano's] detention," say authors Jerre Mangione and Ben Morreale in their book *La Storia,* "the widow sent her Rochester relatives a cry for help. 'I have spent every day and night crying,' she wrote, 'racking my brain hopelessly trying to find a way of escaping this hell. . . . What if they send me back to Italy? Oh God, what should I do? I am here desperate with poor Fortunata who keeps on crying and asking when we can leave this place.'"

The letter convinced Alfano's sister-in-law that the situation was urgent. She returned to Ellis Island, this time with her husband. They brought along his credentials, including a bankbook that showed he could afford to support Alfano and her daughter until she found employment. Satisfied, immigration authorities released the two into his custody.

Interpreters didn't always speak the same dialects as the immigrants. Conversation, especially in a foreign language, could be difficult to hear in the crowded, noisy Great Hall. Some immigrants received their own first names as last names. For example, an employee who was having trouble communicating with an arrival might hear a family member call him Angelo and mistakenly record him as Mr. Angelo. Because few of the immigrants could read and write in Italian, let alone English, they rarely caught such mistakes until later. Even those who knew a mistake had been made were reluctant to correct an official who had the power to deport them.

As problematic as a name might be, the trickiest question of all was the one that asked if the immigrant had a job lined up in the United States. To this question, the seemingly obvious answer, "Yes," was the wrong one. U.S. law prohibited firms from signing labor agreements with prospective immigrants while they were still overseas. The goal was to prevent corrupt business owners from taking advantage of newcomers before they learned how things worked. However, a flat "No" was also a suspect response. An immigrant without a job might be deported as a potential drain on public resources. The best answers sounded something like this: "Not

Even though there were many hurdles, most immigrants who arrived at Ellis Island were allowed to enter the United States.

the women's hands. They assumed that a woman without calluses on her hands was not used to hard work and therefore suspect. Such women were detained until officials could contact their U.S. sponsors and verify their credentials.

Leaving the Island

Despite all the obstacles, 75 to 80 percent of immigrants passing through Ellis Island completed the process without problems. Most of the rest were detained for a short time and eventually allowed to enter the country. Among Italians, the numbers were even more encouraging, largely because of the Italian government's mandate for more comprehensive preboarding physical exams than other countries required.

Once the newcomers had finished running the gauntlet of doctors, inspectors, and clerks, they were free to go. Authors Morreale and Carola describe the final step in the process: "They [the immigrants] were told to walk down a corridor to a door bearing the simple, yet emotion-filled sign, 'Push. To New York.' Indeed, they would find that to make it in New York they would have to push. For now, they felt a moment of relief as they passed through the door to the cheering reception of waiting friends and relatives, and then there was yet another ferry ride for their long-awaited trip to Manhattan—*lamerica*—or, guided by immigration officials, to a train that would take them to some other destination."[31] Finally, the new Americans had arrived.

yet, but I have likely prospects," or "No, but my cousin is recommending me to his boss."

Unmarried women faced special scrutiny by officials at Ellis Island. The officials wanted to satisfy themselves that the women would not become public charges and were not prostitutes. Some inspectors asked to see

CHAPTER FIVE

On the Job in the United States

On the whole, Italian immigrants—men, women, and children—were a hardworking group, accustomed to poverty and poor working conditions. Michael D'Innocenzo, a history professor and the son of Italian immigrants, says, "I'm so impressed by Italians in general, about the work ethic, the dignity of labor, the honoring of sweat and physical effort. In our community, people would look at your hands. When we were growing up they kind of would make fun of the younger generation and say, 'Look! Look at your hands. What kind of calluses do you have?' The worst thing you could be was not poor but lazy."[32]

In an effort to support themselves and their families, many immigrants found difficult and sometimes dangerous jobs in factories, in mines, on farms, and in other businesses throughout the country. Some arrived with such jobs already secured. Others arrived in the United States and began looking for work right away. Most found it quickly; jobs were plentiful for those who didn't mind hard work.

Off the Farm

Despite their backgrounds in agricultural work, most Italians eschewed farming in America, in part because the constant uncertainties and mind-numbing poverty common to rural life in the Mezzogiorno had disillusioned them. Also, farming required money to invest in land and equipment and to pay for the railroad fare to the countryside, money that most Italian immigrants did not have. Furthermore, rural Italians were accustomed to living in small, intimate hill towns, close to their fellow villagers, and walking to the fields, far outside the towns. In the United States, farm families lived on large, isolated properties, far from their neighbors, few of whom were Italian.

For the most part, says one writer, the new immigrants

were unprepared, linguistically and temperamentally, to venture out into the wide open spaces that had already been homesteaded largely by Irish, Germans, and Swedes, and, of course, by native-born American frontiersmen and gunslingers who had little fondness for foreigners. . . . The Italians preferred the protective insularity of ghettos, where their dialect could be understood, where they could buy imported Italian sausage and olive oil. . . . And when the imports from Italy began including women, they began to nurture their families in towering crowded tenements that in a strange way evoked the mountain village atmosphere that had surrounded them from birth.[33]

Most Italian immigrants settled in cities where their neighbors spoke the same language and where they had access to traditional foods.

So instead of farming, most Italian immigrants settled in cities and company towns. Most of the opportunities there—for men, women, and children without special skills—came in the form of grueling jobs with long hours and pay that was low by U.S. standards. But the work was plentiful and steady.

Factory Work

Factory work of all kinds was popular among Italian immigrants, especially women, who had fewer options than men because mining companies, railroads, and construction firms would not hire them. Factories offered jobs for skilled and unskilled immigrants, but most of the southern Italians filled the unskilled slots; few had specialized job experience. Such work was often repetitive and dangerous, and took place in overcrowded, poorly ventilated buildings.

Many of the women worked in textile factories, where they hunched over sewing machines, looms, or other equipment from dawn until dark. Ralph DeRicci's first wife, Norma Tomassoni, was making pants at a clothing factory when the couple met. Tomassoni, like most factory workers, was hired on a "piece-work" basis, which meant that instead of a set salary, she received a certain amount of money for every item—in her case, every pair of pants—she completed. In some industries, workers brought additional work home with them for their families to help with, for which they were also paid by the piece.

As a result of growing industrialization, certain parts of the northeastern United States became centers for factory work, so they attracted the new Italian Americans who were eager for jobs. Massachusetts, for example, was known for its enormous textile factories. Upstate New York, a popular spot for a variety of manufacturing industries, also became a destination for arriving Italian immigrants. Endicott-Johnson, a shoe manufacturer based there, had originally defied the antirecruitment law by sending agents to Italy to contract with likely workers there. Soon, the company found a more efficient, legal recruitment method: Managers simply told Italian American employees that they needed workers. The employees convinced so many of their friends and relatives to journey from Italy to seek jobs there that the firm was able to stop all of its overseas contracting. According to historians, "So effective was the new process of chain migration in supplying laborers to Endicott-Johnson, that legend has it that the first words that Italians uttered when they disembarked in New York was, 'Which-a-way, E-J?'"[34]

"All the Men from Italy Worked in the Mines"

Large numbers of Italian men found work in mines and rock quarries. They gravitated toward these occupations because many had experience working with stone. For generations they had lived in Italy's rocky hill towns, where they had cut and shaped stone in order to build and repair their homes and other structures. Many had worked in Sicily's sulfur mines, too, often from early childhood.

Although the more skilled among them sculpted and crafted in marble and granite, most immigrant men who labored in rock trooped into the mines every morning, where the work was dangerous, dirty, and uncomfortable. "My father . . . worked in the mines,"

Mary Piccioli (later Ciabocchi), whose father, Fortunato, was one of the many Italian immigrants who worked in rock quarries and mines.

says Mary Ciabocchi of her father, Fortunato Piccioli. "There was nothing else for them to do; all the men from Italy worked in the mines."[35] Mining dominated the economy in northeastern Pennsylvania, where the Picciolis lived, because of the rich veins of anthracite, a type of coal, that marbled the rock underlying the land. Men from throughout Europe, especially Italy and Poland, toiled underground to extract the coal. Women, however, never worked in the mines, because of a deep-seated superstition among miners that a woman in a mine would bring bad luck.

Even without women underground, many miners seemed destined for bad luck. After all, their daily work was fraught with appalling perils, including contact with poisonous gases and cave-ins. One mine worker describes a terrifying cave-in: "I was about a mile underground. I could hear the timbers squeezing and breaking as I loaded the car up. . . . All of a sudden, twenty feet from me, *boom!* [The roof] started coming down and pushed the sides in. I got caught under a big rock, and I couldn't get out. My leg was broken. There I was, all alone. No light. Complete darkness . . . for five or six hours. I lay there, waiting. Finally, the rescuers got to me and carried me out on a stretcher."[36]

Many miners were killed or permanently injured in mine collapses. Ralph DeRicci's family lived in Scranton, Pennsylvania, where his father-in-law, Anthony Tomassoni, toiled in the mines to help support his family. Like so many others, Tomassoni died in a mining accident. He was twenty-five years old and left behind a pregnant wife and three small children. Other miners retired from their years in the mines apparently unscathed, only to succumb later to black lung, a deadly disease contracted from breathing coal dust.

Pennsylvania wasn't the only place where Italians mined the earth. As far away as California and even Alaska, Italian Americans mined for gold and various minerals. In fact, in 1915, the Alaska Gold Mines Company reported that almost 8 percent of the workers at its Alaska Gastineau mine were Italian-born.

Westward Expansion

Eighty percent of Italian immigrants in America chose to remain east of the Mississippi. In fact, the 1900 census showed that 72 percent of all Italian immigrants lived in New England, New York, New Jersey, and Pennsylvania. But others continued west, especially to California, where many of them chose to work in farms, in orchards, or in vineyards. Sunny California was their destination of choice because the climate and landscape were similar to those of Italy but had conditions better suited to farming.

Another draw was California's commercial fishing industry. The immigrants were used to living around the water; Italy is a narrow peninsula that juts into the Mediterranean. In some families, fishing had been the mainstay for generations until overharvesting depleted the supply of fish, forcing many Italians to turn to other occupations. The waters off California, on the other hand, still teemed with fish.

Joseph Alioto, who later became the mayor of San Francisco, grew up in a family that helped pioneer the fishing industry at that city's famous Fisherman's Wharf. "My father said we were fishermen in Sicily. And then the fish in the Mediterranean got depleted, and they came to America. They went to where the jobs were, in San Francisco." The Aliotos worked side by side with other Italian immigrants. Like most Italian families who owned their own boats, they hired fellow Italians to fish on their crews. "My dad's company had approximately eight boats," remembers Alioto. "And many of his *paesani* from the same village in Sicily did the actual fishing."[37]

Fishing and farming also lured Italian Americans to Louisiana, which around 1900 became a popular destination for Sicilians

Some Italians moved to California to work in vineyards and on farms.

Alaska Gold: The Story of Felix Pedro

Italian-born miner Felix Pedro kept moving across the United States in search of work that fulfilled his longing for adventure and his quest to prove himself as a first-class miner. He was born Felice Pedroni in 1858 in Trignano di Fanano, in the mountains of northern Italy, the last of six children in an uneducated peasant family. At age twenty-three he immigrated, alone, to the United States; his first job was in Peoria, Illinois. Over the next decade, Pedro continued to travel west, working as a farmhand in Indian territory and in the silver and coal mines of Colorado, Utah, and Oregon.

Eventually, Pedro ended up in Alaska, where after years of analyzing the landscape and panning the streams, he became the first person to discover gold in what is now the Fairbanks area.

Pedro became head of a mining consortium and grew to be wealthy, but he was always more interested in the challenge of the search and the thrill of the find. Today, everyone in Fairbanks has heard of Felix Pedro. A mountain and a stream are named after him. Pedroni couldn't read or write even in Italian, let alone English. So he never realized that his fellow Alaskans, stumped by his accent, had recorded his name incorrectly.

who wanted to leave the eastern seaboard. Most settled first in farming communities and later moved to the cities, where they began to play a central role in food-related industries. One example was the Taormina family and their cousins the Uddos, who began by picking vegetables by hand. Today, the New Orleans–based canned-goods company they founded, Progresso, still cans soups, sauces, beans, and other products for a national market.

Life in the Midwest

Other Italian Americans ventured inland and settled in the Midwest, where they worked for the same kinds of companies that employed their fellow immigrants in New York and Pennsylvania. The story of Giovanni (John) Musacchio is typical. Musacchio left Italy in 1905, bound for New York, but soon continued inland to join his brother Gus, who had immigrated to Chicago. Musacchio found a job with the Illinois Central Railroad. Says his niece, "He started as a water boy, trailing the gangs that laid and repaired track on the still expanding American rail network. As a new arrival he was the lowest person on the crew, and earned meager wages of a few pennies an hour. But those few pennies, multiplied by long hours of labor, were enough for John to pay for his lodgings and send money back home."[38]

Although Chicago was by far the most popular midwestern city for Italian Americans, it was by no means the only one. The newly industrialized city of Cleveland, Ohio, with its abundant jobs, was another destination of choice. According to Edward

During the early 1900s, it was common for immigrant children to work on farms, in factories, and in mines.

D'Alessandro, whose immigrant father moved to Cleveland from New York City in 1900,

> The Otis Steel Company had taken over the valley [Ohio's Cuyahoga River valley] and filled it with huge blast furnaces with towering smoke stacks that belched grey, ghostlike smoke during the day while adjacent appendages spewed orange-colored flames at night. The Baltimore and Ohio and the Wheeling and Lake Erie Railway Companies had brought in their shiny rails to serve the steel makers and the passenger trade of the growing industrial metropolis on the shores of Lake Erie. The steel and railway companies were attracting large numbers of Italian immigrants.[39]

Some immigrants preferred the Midwest, mainly because it wasn't as crowded as New York City, where most of them had started out. With space at less of a premium, immigrants could rent larger, more comfortable, and more affordable apartments than the ones

Many children of immigrants left school at a young age, including Ralph DeRicci (pictured).

"Nobody Cared If You Didn't Go to School"

Whether in the East, Midwest, or elsewhere, instead of attending school, many immigrant children—some as young as five years old—worked full-time jobs to help support their families. Just to survive, many families needed every family member to earn a salary. Others aspired to upward mobility, which required more than just getting by; it required savings.

Work, though, was not the only reason so many immigrant children did not attend school. Another reason was cultural. Many southern Italians never even considered the notion of educating their children. They had come from a society in which illiteracy was the norm. Among poor families of the Mezzogiorno, childhood was short. By the age of ten, many children were treated like miniature adults and expected to take on adult-size responsibilities.

Ralph DeRicci, son of Italian immigrants, says he left school in the fifth grade, but not because his parents pressured him to. "In those days, nobody cared if you didn't go to school. I didn't like it. I didn't want to go anymore." Because he chose to drop out, DeRicci's mother insisted that he get a job and turn over his wages to her. First she apprenticed him to a plumber. But the plumber beat him, and DeRicci fled after only a few weeks, walking fifteen miles to get home. Next he found a job at a nuts and bolts factory. Explaining the work, he says,

> You had a basket over here and a basket over here. There was nuts in here and bolts over here, and you grab a bolt and

that could be found in the tenement blocks of Manhattan and Brooklyn. Wherever they lived and worked, though, Italians tended to congregate with other Italians, preferably from their hometowns in the Old Country. So when one Italian moved to a midwestern city, friends and relatives soon followed, hoping for the first settler's help in finding employment.

a nut, and you just start the nut on the bolt . . . and then you used to throw them in a big basket. And they [the bosses] would count them. . . . They'd weigh them, and they could tell how many you'd finished. They used to pay you so much a hundred. You made very little money. Aw, Jesus, it was like peanuts. But I liked it better than going to school.[40]

Girls held full-time jobs, too. One of Ralph's sisters, Philomena, worked in a silk factory as a teenager. In fact, of the family's seven children who survived infancy, only Louie, the youngest, finished high school.

Children worked in a wide variety of industries. In large eastern cities, especially New York, Boston, and Philadelphia, many Italian immigrants apprenticed their children to *padroni,* neighborhood bosses, who sent

Children often had to take on full-time jobs to help their families financially.

them into the streets as peddlers or musicians. Other Italian American children worked in factories; they were the only ones small enough for some of the most dangerous jobs, those that required crawling inside the machinery to adjust settings or fix problems. Children were often injured or killed performing such tasks. Nonetheless, many bragged about the risks they took. They saw the dangerous work as exciting and glamorous.

Children in the Mines

Some of the most grueling jobs available to boys were in mining. An 1885 law set twelve as the minimum age for working in the breakers, where newly mined coal was sorted. Boys had to be fourteen to work in-

side the mines themselves. In 1902, a new law aimed at protecting small children from hazardous work raised the age for breaker boys to fourteen, but parents who needed their sons' earnings often managed to evade the law. "Parents and coal miners found it easy to get around the law in Pennsylvania, which had no compulsory registration of births,"[41] says writer Susan Campbell Bartoletti. Parents could get a certificate from a mine inspector and, for twenty-five cents, have it notarized, verifying that their son was any age they chose. Such deceptions were trickier in states where official records could confirm a boy's date of birth.

Mary Ciabocchi tells a story of a child who was forced to play an adult's role. Her first husband had become a breaker boy at the age of eleven. His parents—who in 1902 had em-

Some children earned money by becoming street peddlers.

igrated from Gubbio, in central Italy—both died on October 9, 1918, in a flu epidemic. Their deaths forced their son to drop out of elementary school and work to support his younger sisters. He soon moved from the breaker into the mine itself, where a group of miners from Poland took an interest in the boy and taught him to speak Polish. He grew up to be president of a miners' union before moving into law enforcement and local politics, eventually becoming mayor of Old Forge, Pennsylvania.

His story is unusual only because of the level of success he achieved after such inauspicious beginnings. The responsibilities he took on as a child, however, were quite common. In the days before Social Security, health insurance, and other support systems that protect today's families from disaster, the children of Italian immigrants were often forced to step into adult roles in troubled times. Some mining companies even claimed to offer their workers a kind of unofficial "life insurance": If a coal miner died, the company guaranteed a job for his son, ensuring that the family would still have at least one wage earner.

Arts and Crafts

Not all Italian immigrants endured the difficult lives of day laborers. The new Americans also included artists, skilled tradespeople, and musicians. This was especially true among those who came from Italy's northern provinces, where people were more likely to be educated. The peak emigration period from those regions was earlier, during a time when travel restrictions still kept southern Italians in their villages. Chicago, for in-

Italians who were skilled in a trade sometimes avoided backbreaking labor by opening their own shops.

stance, boasted a community of early Italian immigrants, some of whom had been there since the early and mid–nineteenth century. Many of these Italian Chicagoans—especially those from Genoa, a northern Italian port town and bustling trade center—were merchants.

Some skilled tradespeople, like writer Gay Talese's father, Joseph, sewed clothing—not in factories on complex machines but by hand, with painstaking attention to every stitch. Tailors like Joseph brought their trade to the United States, where many eventually opened their own shops.

Italians also had a long tradition of excellence in the fine arts. Many of the early immigrants from northern Italy continued that tradition in the United States. In Washington, D.C., the U.S. Capitol building was decorated

Bringing Stone to Life

For centuries, Italy's rocky terrain and the necessity to rebuild after frequent earthquakes created some of the world's finest stone masons and carvers. Many brought their skills with them to the New World. One of these was Vincent Palumbo, who first picked up a chisel at the age of nine in his family's workshop in Malfetta, Italy.

After immigrating to Washington, D.C., Palumbo worked alongside his father, Paolo, first on the restoration of the U.S. Capitol building and then at the National Cathedral. In his decades at the cathedral, Palumbo carved thousands of pieces of stone for both the interior and the exterior. He created flowers, leaves, gargoyles, angels, and a variety of figures, including the large statues of St. Peter and St. Paul that grace the cathedral's main entrance. In 1978, Vincent Palumbo was named cathedral master carver, a post he held until his death in December 2000.

in large part by Italian-born painters, sculptors, and stone carvers, whom the U.S. government brought to America for that purpose. One early immigrant, sculptor Giuseppi Franzoni, traveled to the United States in 1806 to sculpt statues and other stonework for the Capitol; congressmen praised his work for its "truly American"[42] qualities. Another immigrant Constantine Brumidi, who came to America in 1852, became a U.S. citizen in 1854 and spent the next twenty-five years painting murals and other art works inside the Capitol.

Music was another area of the arts in which Italian immigrants found employment. From the lowliest organ grinders to world-famous Italian American tenor Enrico Caruso, some Italian-born Americans made a living making music. And skilled artists brought music to America in a different way by crafting musical instruments.

Pride in a Job Well Done

Whatever kind of work they found, early Italian immigrants as a group earned a reputation for hard work and high standards. Whether musicians or masons, farmers or factory workers, most took pride in their work, for the Italian culture prized all kinds of work from manual labor to fine art. And few Italians were raised to think of menial tasks as beneath them.

That attitude of pride is illustrated by Kaye Ballard, an actress best known for her starring role in the 1960s television series *The Mothers-In-Law*. Ballard was born Catherine Gloria Balotta, the daughter of Italian immigrants. She describes her father's respect for his work: "My father came to Cleveland. Since he was a cement finisher he would take me around town and say, 'I put that sidewalk down in 1933. You see *that?* I put *that* sidewalk down in 1939.' He was so proud of the work he did."[43] It was pride in a job well done—along with hope for a brighter future—that kept many immigrants going, even through the days of heavy labor, child exploitation, mine cave-ins, and appalling working conditions. Most Italians felt grateful to have work and were determined to make the most of it.

CHAPTER SIX

Creating Little Italy

In all walks of life, Italian immigrants set about to replicate their Italian village life in their new surroundings. Many settled together in communities that were made up not just of fellow Italians but of Italians who had been neighbors in their hometowns. In smog-choked Pennsylvania mining settlements, in the hills of California, in midwestern steel-mill towns, and in run-down blocks of Brooklyn tenements, the immigrants listened to Caruso, planted tomatoes, crushed grapes into wine, and celebrated the feasts of the saints.

Greenies

Until they felt settled and could afford to bring other family members across the ocean, newly arrived immigrants, called greenies, often stayed with friends or relatives who had immigrated earlier. According to Mary Ciabocchi, it seemed that "every greenie that came from Italy came to board at my mother's house. Friends from the country where my parents came from—they came there and paid rent."[44] Typically, she says, the boarders were former neighbors, who had just arrived from her parents' hometown of Serravalle. Eventually they moved out to start their own households, either marrying local Italian women or bringing over the wives they had left in Italy.

Ralph DeRicci's family also took in newly arrived immigrants as boarders, but they were always relatives. Often, DeRicci's father would help the men get work on the railroad at which he was employed. "It's something, how these people would leave Europe and come to this country," DeRicci says. "It's hard. The only way was you had to have a relative or something to sponsor you, and they'd give you a place to stay. And then you would pay them back, and you would stay there until you got enough money to go off on your own."[45]

The *Padrone* System

Some of the early immigrants who sponsored later arrivals built power bases for themselves,

becoming padroni, or bosses. ("*Padroni*" is plural; the singular is "*padrone*.") Padroni were the American incarnation of *gabelloti*, the opportunistic overseers who had worked for the wealthy landowners back in Italy. In early twentieth-century New York, padroni controlled two-thirds of Italian laborers. Fluent in English as well as Italian, better educated than the average peasant, and filled with entrepreneurial spirit, padroni acted as a liaisons between non-English-speaking immigrants and the often perplexing institutions of the United States.

Padroni played many roles. They acted as travel agents, cutting through the required paperwork to bring Italians to America. They

Italian immigrants tended to congregate in cities and communities with people who had been their neighbors in Italy.

found immigrants jobs and rooms to rent, handled their banking needs, wrote letters home for them, and sometimes provided food and clothing. The most influential padroni owned their own businesses, for which they hired greenies as employees.

Some padroni had honorable intentions and sought to provide important services to their fellow Italians. They helped the newcomers get established, taught them what they needed to know about their new country, translated for them, and protected them from people who might take advantage of their naivete. In the process, these padroni created communities of Italian Americans who clustered around them in what became "Little Italy" sections of many cities.

Most padroni, though, were opportunistic and shamelessly exploited the vulnerable new arrivals. They charged the newcomers a fee for finding them jobs and then charged the employer for finding workers. They demanded commissions of as much as 60 percent of the workers' wages and charged fees for transportation to the work site. They also demanded exorbitant interest rates on loans. Workers were afraid to rebel against them because the padroni threatened to have them arrested if they tried. And the padroni set up the new arrivals in overcrowded, unsanitary living conditions.

Danish immigrant, writer, and reformer Jacob Riis reported on slums in the Bend, a major Italian neighborhood located in Lower Manhattan's Mulberry Street district. He described conditions in one tenement block in the late nineteenth century, exactly the kind of place where padroni would have secured sleeping space for their charges. The 132 rooms housed 1,324 Italian immigrants, most

Many Italian immigrants lived in overcrowded tenements like New York City's Mulberry Bend (pictured).

of them male Sicilian laborers who slept in tiers of bunks. Riis describes "one room 12 [feet] x 12 [feet] with five families living in it, comprising twenty persons of both sexes and all ages, with only two beds, without partitions, screen, chair or table."[46] Fortunately, such conditions did not last long. In 1901 the city demolished the worst of the Mulberry Bend tenements and created a park there.

Fortunately for the greenies, a padrone's control did not last indefinitely. Typically, an immigrant would remain under an exploitative padrone's influence for about two years. That's generally how long it took to learn enough about the United States—and enough English—to realize that other options existed.

Poor living conditions were commonplace for immigrants in New York City, a result of the high demand for housing and landlords' lack of concern for renovations.

Poor Living Conditions

Even immigrants who were not controlled by dishonorable padroni often lived in places that were considered uninhabitable by most Americans' standards. Plumbing didn't work. Mold grew on the ceilings. And many apartments received almost no natural light. Especially in eastern cities, diseases such as influenza and tuberculosis claimed many lives in the crowded and unsanitary tenements. Furthermore, in the dark and stifling rear tenements, it was not uncommon for a third of all the babies born there to die in their first year.

One reason for these problems was that the enormous influx of European immigrants had outpaced the number of apartments being built, especially in New York where so many Ellis Island arrivals settled. A little before the turn of the twentieth century, city officials reported that, of the 4,367 apartments in Mulberry Bend, only 9 were vacant. With so many people and so few affordable spaces, rooms were in great demand. Landlords could rent even substandard ones, so they had little incentive to renovate.

Despite this kind of poverty, the Italian immigrants seldom resorted to taking government handouts. They were one of the poorest immigrant groups in New York, but they were used to being poor. They were also resourceful. They picked through people's trash for usable items, especially rags, which could be sold to paper manufacturers for recycling. Some Italian immigrants even paid Irish workers on garbage scows—barges that transported garbage away from the city—to let them take over the job of spreading the garbage evenly over the barges. That way, they could scavenge anything useful from the trash.

The immigrants did those things because most believed in one key difference between the United States and the Mezzogiorno: In

America, they could pull themselves out of their poverty. In fact, within a year of passing through Ellis Island, most immigrants had moved themselves into better jobs and housing than they had when they arrived. For example, immigrant Rocco D'Alessandro began his life in the United States with three months in the sweatshops of New York's garment district. In 1900, as soon as he'd saved enough money, D'Alessandro moved to Cleveland to join friends from Italy who had relocated there. He settled in a three-story brick tenement house built by real estate tycoons Henry and John Newcomb. Six years later he sent for his wife and son to join him there.

The D'Alessandros' Cleveland home was typical of the kind of place where immigrants might live as they began working their way up in American society. "The Newcomb Block, as it was first known, contained twenty-seven four-room flats [apartments]," explains Rocco's son, Edward D'Alessandro. "Each flat had a large kitchen because the Newcomb brothers had learned that the Italians liked big kitchens."[47] Unlike the worst tenement blocks in New York, each apartment had its own bathroom, which consisted of a tiny closet with a flush toilet. The only sink was in the kitchen.

Company Towns and Free Towns

Living conditions in other industrial cities were similar, although upon arrival, newcomers usually did live in poverty for a time.

Angel of Mercy: The Italian American Saint

The survival of Italian communities depended on immigrants helping each other. One person who did more than almost anyone to help the most disadvantaged immigrants was an Italian-born nun, Sister Frances Xavier Cabrini.

Cabrini immigrated to the United States in 1889 and became a U.S. citizen in 1909. She began her ministry in New Orleans, helping to heal the emotional wounds caused by a mass lynching of Italian Americans there in 1891. In New Orleans, she founded a missionary group, the Missionary Sisters of the Sacred Heart, and with the help of the four thousand sisters she recruited, Cabrini took her crusade nationwide. She ministered to people of all ethnic backgrounds, but her special interest was in helping her fellow Italians.

Altogether, Cabrini founded fourteen colleges, ninety-eight schools, twenty-eight orphanages, eight hospitals, three training centers, and a score of other institutions. A semi-invalid herself, Cabrini ministered tirelessly to the sick, disabled, poor, persecuted, and unemployed until her death in 1917. In 1946, Mother Cabrini, as she was called, became the first American to be canonized, or recognized as a saint by the Catholic Church.

In these places, immigrants often lived in company towns, settlements that grew up around a business and were owned by that business. Thus, many workers were dependent on their employer not only for their jobs but for their homes as well.

One such company town, Ambler, Pennsylvania, was the site of an asbestos manufacturing firm, Keasbey and Mattison Company, which hired newly arrived Italians to work in the asbestos quarry or to serve as apprentice stone masons and artisans. Many of these laborers lived in two large boardinghouses owned by padrone Carmine Lobianco, an overseer for the company. The boardinghouses accommodated single men or men who had left their wives and children behind in Italy until they could afford to send for them. The men slept on cornhusk mattresses, with four bunks crammed into each small room. As they worked at the firm longer and saved up enough to pay higher rent—and especially after their families joined them in Ambler—many workers moved to a more comfortable form of company housing in an area of simple stone row houses and frame buildings in the company's Italian quarter.

Similar arrangements were found in company towns all over the East and Midwest, where lodging was provided by the coal companies, factories, and textile mills that employed the workers. These accommodations usually took the form of company houses, boardinghouses, or dormitories. Many were hastily thrown-together structures that were little better than shacks. Rents, sometimes exorbitant ones, were deducted from workers' wages. In coal country, these company towns were called "patch villages," and the company owned not just mining facilities and worker accommodations, but everything: the company store where families bought all their groceries and supplies, often at unfair prices; the church; the school; and even the police department. "The patch village was laid out according to the class of worker," says writer Susan Campbell Bartoletti.

At the head of the streets, the mine bosses and supervisors lived in large, comfortable homes. Next came the miners' houses, which usually had two rooms. . . . Thin pieces of wood were nailed over the outside seams but did little to keep out the rain and the cold. . . . Outhouses, usually shared by at least two families, stood in the backyards. Chickens, dogs, cats, pigs, and goats ran free.[48]

Other mines and factories were located near "free towns," such as Scranton, Pennsylvania. The companies did not own these towns and were not the sole employers there, although bigger companies did wield a lot of influence. Still, workers with enough money could buy their own homes in a free town, lessening their dependence on their employers.

In remote areas, Italian miners and railroad workers lived in bunkhouses, tents, or railway cars. A report on the building of the Alaska railroads from 1915 to 1923 describes living conditions for the workers there, many of whom were Italian immigrants: "There was no smiling camp steward to direct the new arrivals to their quarters. The new arrivals generally had to provide or build their own. In some areas log cabins chinked with moss

Some Italian immigrant railroad workers lived in "free towns" and did not depend on their employers for housing.

were hastily constructed. . . . Empty flour sacks covered the openings where windows should have been. The bunks were made out of poles, like honeycomb cells at both ends of the building, similar in arrangement to post office boxes."[49] In addition to being their bunkhouses, such accommodations also served the workers as cook houses, storerooms, dining rooms, and social halls.

Picking Coal

Like the garbage-scow scavengers of New York, Italians in smaller cities and towns learned to be resourceful, an education that began at an early age. For example, among children who lived in coal-mining regions, a typical chore for girls and boys of all ages was "picking coal." To pick coal, the children climbed on the local culm banks—mountainous heaps of rocky rubble that

were by-products of coal extraction—and sifted through the rocks in search of usable chunks of coal.

Picking coal was dangerous. To begin with, the rocky debris underfoot was unstable. If it began to slide as children walked over it, the pickers could be buried alive. Other times, discarded mining supplies caused problems. Mary Ciabocchi, the daughter of immigrants, tells of the tragedy that befell her brother Harry when he was about eight years old. "Harry and I were picking coal one day and we found a red box, and it was locked and we didn't know what was in it. We brought it home and we wanted to see what was inside. Well, my mother called me away and I told Harry to wait for me, but he was impatient. He hit it with a rock to open it."[50] The box was filled with mining explosives, which blew up in the boy's face, leaving Harry permanently blind.

Coal pickers risked lesser hazards as well. From the coal company's perspective, picking coal was stealing. Culm banks were trash, but they were the company's trash. "The culm banks were guarded by the company police," says Bartoletti. "Some police looked the other way, but others smashed the pickers' baskets, wagons, and wheelbarrows. Some even searched the mine workers' homes for evidence of picked coal. If found out, the families had to pay fines and pay for the coal."[51]

Italian Insularity

Despite the dangers and poverty, immigrants in both company towns and big cities chose to remain close together in ghettos and tenements because they felt at home there. Traditionally, Italian villagers were clannish. Centuries of oppression and invading armies had nurtured a deep distrust of outsiders. Travel restrictions under the Bourbon rulers and the variations in Italian dialects had reinforced their insularity. Immigrants brought that mind-set with them to the United States.

Some Italians tried to live among non-Italians, but the established residents considered the newcomers too foreign because of their unfamiliar language, typically dark coloring, unusual foods, and Catholic faith. Tales of discrimination filtered back to the immigrants who remained in Italian American enclaves in towns and cities, and most felt justified in their decision to live among their *paesani* (people from the same homeland).

This isolation from mainstream America led to misunderstandings. For instance, among other Americans, the Italian immigrants gained a reputation for not caring about social and political issues, in part because many didn't become American citizens for years, lagging behind other immigrant groups. In reality, though, many Italian Americans were simply too busy trying to feed their families to think about politics. Others delayed citizenship because they couldn't read well enough or because they still counted on returning to Italy someday. By far, the most widespread reason the immigrants didn't bother with citizenship was that they had no frame of reference for it since for centuries, Italy had been a collection of regions, not a unified political entity. Because they didn't think of themselves as Italian citizens, it didn't occur to many of them to become United States citizens.

A rooted distrust of outsiders kept many Italians from living in areas populated by non-Italians.

Thus, during the early years of the peak immigration period, the communities the immigrants worked for were not the cities they lived in but their own Italian American neighborhoods, extensions of the villages of their birth. Within these communities, Italian-run organizations operated schools, libraries, and aid societies where immigrants helped each other to get started in their new homeland and then advance and prosper.

Little Italy, U.S.A.

Within these neighborhoods, immigrants recreated the sights, sounds, and smells of their homeland. "I grew up in a neighborhood where everyone spoke Italian," says Jerry Della Femina. "The radio station was . . . the Italian radio station. The newspaper we read was *Il Progresso* [America's largest Italian-language newspaper]. I thought I was in Italy."[52] Little Italy sections sprang up in cities such as Boston, Philadelphia, Chicago, Baltimore, and San Francisco. During the late 1800s, the famous French Quarter in New Orleans was so heavily Italian that it was called Little Palermo, named after a city in Sicily. But by far the biggest Italian population was in New York City.

Italian culture flourished in the boroughs of New York. "Bruculinu, as the Sicilian immigrants called their Brooklyn neighborhood, was a remarkable place," says Italian American actor Vincent Schiavelli, who grew up there.

The old three- and four-story tenement houses overflowed with new arrivals. Whole families, in some places practically the population of whole towns,

Paesano, Can You Lend a Dime?

Italians couldn't build communities without money, but at the turn of the twentieth century, most banks shunned Italian immigrants, refusing to offer them home mortgages or other credit. Without bank loans, it was difficult to start a business and emerge from the cycle of poverty that kept Italians in blue-collar jobs.

In response, two Italians who had become successful themselves worked to bring their compatriots into the mainstream of American life. Thomas Marinelli (also known as Thomas Marnell) began in America as a construction foreman. By 1890 he had opened the Italian Exchange Bank in Syracuse, New York, to help immigrants start their own businesses and buy homes. He was so well respected among Italians that many considered his word final in any kind of personal or financial dispute.

In San Francisco, Amadeo Giannini opened the Bank of Italy in 1904 to provide collateral-free loans to Italian immigrants. These loans saved many Italians from financial ruin after they lost everything in the San Francisco earthquake of 1906. Giannini's bank grew into Bank of America, one of the largest banks in the world.

In large cities, Little Italy sections emerged, providing a wealth of Italian culture, food, and shops.

were clustered in particular buildings and streets. It was not uncommon to see the latest arrivals, with their bundles, trying to find the residence of a cousin in America, their only reference an address on a slip of paper held tightly in hand. . . . If the weather was fair, the streets themselves would be teeming with life. Women would be haggling with push-cart vendors in Sicilian and broken English over prices of fruits and vegetables. Other vendors in horse-drawn wagons would be chanting their wares, amid the sound of the ragman's bell and the ice-man's bellow. . . . [Growing up in Bruculinu] was like having one foot in mid-twentieth-century United States and the other in mid-sixteenth-century Sicily.[53]

The Role of the Church

Roman Catholic churches played a central role in the life of Italian immigrants after 1900. Until then, the church had been run mainly by priests with Irish backgrounds, and Italian immigrants didn't always feel welcome. As more Italians settled in the United States, the numbers of Italian priests grew as well. Italian neighborhoods established their own parishes with Italian American priests, parishes where they could worship in ways that felt comfortable for them. Even today, many northeastern towns with large Catholic populations still have churches commonly known as the Irish Church and the Italian Church.

In the early days of Italian immigration, differences in styles of worship between

Italian Catholics and Irish Catholics often led to tension between the two groups. Italian Americans showed their faith more externally and emotionally than Irish Americans. For instance, they placed more emphasis on the saints. In particular, Italians honored the patron saints of their cities and villages back in Italy, often with large, enthusiastic processions through the streets of their new American cities. Authors Ben Morreale and Robert Carola describe the *festas,* or feasts of the saints, as New York Italians celebrated them during the Ellis Island era:

"A favorite festival in the Mulberry district honored Saint Rocco, revered among southern Italians for his miraculous cures of the diseased and maimed. Paraders reminded spectators of Saint Rocco's miracles by carrying wax arms, legs, hands, and other parts of the body. San Gennaro, the patron saint of Naples, was a huge favorite,

---

Magic and Mysticism

Some southern Italian immigrants peppered their sometimes fierce Catholicism with an ancient brand of superstitious mysticism that evolved over thousands of years amid the rocky hills of the Mezzogiorno.

In *The Ginney Block: Reminiscences of an Italian-American Dead-End Street Kid,* Edward D'Alessandro tells the story of an elderly, black-garbed woman who lived in flat number one of his building, which was called the Ginney Block. "As one of many children in the Ginney Block, I was destined to be treated by Maria di Maria, faith healer and Dispeller of the evil eye." D'Alessandro says that one day he had a terrible headache, and his mother was convinced that a neighbor had placed the evil eye on him. The evil eye, *il malocchio* in Italian, is a curse. To remove the curse, D'Alessandro's mother escorted him downstairs to Maria's flat.

"Without a word, Maria nodded and walked to the cupboard over the kitchen sink," he recalls. "She brought forth an ancient saucer, which was chipped around the edge. She then produced a can of olive oil from a lower cupboard. Fascinated, I watched her pour about one teaspoonful of oil along with some water into the saucer. From a pocket in her black apron, she fished a large door key that looked like a jail door key. I could see that she was now ready for me. . . . She dipped the key in the mixture of water and oil and raised it, dripping the oily mixture to my forehead, and with her fat, pudgy right hand proceeded to make the sign of the cross between my eyebrows."

The visit concluded with his mother's payment of Maria's twenty-five-cent fee. D'Alessandro never mentions whether the treatment cured his headache.

and even today the Feast of San Gennaro in New York's Little Italy draws crowds."[54]

Bella Musica

Religion was only one element of their culture that immigrants re-created in Little Italy neighborhoods across the United States. Many other elements of Italian life have transcended the boundaries of ethnic neighborhoods and become entrenched in the American culture. Of those, the most important are music and food.

Italian musicians in America date back to the days of Thomas Jefferson, who in 1805 recruited a group of fourteen musicians from Italy to form the nucleus of what would become the U.S. Marine band. The most important music to Italian Americans during the peak immigration period was opera. Today, Americans think of opera as music for the rich, well-educated classes, but during the late nineteenth and early twentieth centuries, even the poorest illiterate immigrants cherished the music of Italian opera. Pennsylvania coal miner Anthony Tomassoni, for instance, was an amateur horn player who named his first three children after characters in Italian operas: Norma, Romeo, and Aida. And at the turn of the twentieth century, says author Andrew Rolle, the manager of the San Francisco opera house never had to worry about a shortage of voices to swell the chorus. When the manager lacked singers, "he would send a messenger racing down to the wharves of North Beach [a section of the city], since all the Sicilian fishermen there knew the score of [operas] *La Traviata* or *Rigoletto* by heart."[55]

Italian Americans idolized Italian opera singers, especially the world's most famous opera singer of the time, Enrico Caruso. To the immigrants, Caruso not only symbolized all that was beautiful in their native culture but also stood as an example of what an Italian of humble beginnings could achieve. Born in 1873, Caruso grew up in working-class Naples. The eighteenth of his parents' twenty-one children, he was the first to live past infancy. Caruso began singing as a child and joined a professional opera company in his twenties. There he astonished audiences with the beauty and power of his voice and his unique style. In 1903 he moved to the United States, where he headlined New York's Metropolitan Opera until shortly before his death in 1921. At the peak of his fame, Caruso was

For many Italians, opera singer Enrico Caruso symbolized the possibility of success in America.

the best-selling musical artist in the world. Of course, most Italian immigrants couldn't afford to attend his performances. Instead, they listened at home on gramophones, early devices for playing recorded music.

Feeding Little Italy

While Caruso and other Italian opera singers provided the background music for Little Italy, the background aroma was the smell of cooking. Garlic, tomato sauce, herbed sausages, and pungent cheeses flavored the air. Italians brought their cuisine with them across the ocean, and it was very different from what other Americans were used to. "When I went to school," says Peter Spinogatti, "my mother used to pack me a lunch. Now, the Irish kids had peanut butter and jelly. And I would have . . . all kinds of exotic things emanating from this bag. . . . And in a certain sense I was delighted because it was delicious. On the other hand, [the other children] must have thought I was really weird."[56] Eventually other Americans tried Italian fare and liked it. Today, it has become an integral part of American cooking, with pizza, pasta, and other Italian specialties served in every region of the United States.

To help them re-create the cooking of their homeland and to save money, the immigrants planted gardens, growing much of the same produce they had cultivated in Italy, including tomatoes, basil, eggplants, peppers, fennel, zucchini, and grapes. Even city dwellers with no land would coax vegetables and herbs to grow in pots on windowsills, front stoops, or rooftops. History professor Michael D'Innocenzo explains:

My family . . . had to have a garden. We used every available piece of land to grow vegetables. . . . We grew no flowers. . . . The attitude was why waste land on flowers? You could grow tomatoes. You'd grow peppers. You could grow cucumbers. You could grow lettuce. . . . We grew our own vegetables for two reasons. One, because we got the kinds of products we wanted that were good. And for frugality.[57]

Fig trees were also a common fixture in the yards of Italian immigrants. However, the trees were unsuited to the harsh climate of the northeastern states where so many of the Italian Americans lived. D'Innocenzo says that, in his neighborhood, controversy reigned over the best way to keep the trees alive through the winter. That same argument raged in many Italian enclaves. Some immigrants, like Ralph DeRicci's father, dug up their fig trees in the fall, wrapped them in blankets, and buried them underground until spring, but other fig growers preferred to leave the trees in place for the winter, covering them with rugs for warmth.

To the immigrants, the produce of their homeland—as well as Italian music, religion, and customs—made them feel more at home in an unfamiliar country. The immigrants had chosen to abandon what for many had become an intolerable way of life in Italy, but most refused to abandon their culture. By surrounding themselves with friends and relatives from their ancestral villages and with the sights, smells, tastes, and sounds they remembered from the Old Country, they kept their heritage alive.

CHAPTER SEVEN

Liberty's Broken Promise

Americans once looked to Italy as a cradle of learning and the arts. Gradually, though, they began to revile it as a source of poverty-stricken and illiterate peasants. Even as Italian Americans began to settle into their new communities, it was becoming apparent that many other Americans did not want them there.

Rude Awakenings

By 1880, it was clear that industrialization was changing the way of life in the United States; an agricultural economy had been quickly transformed into an industrial one characterized by rapid growth, overcrowded cities, and labor unrest. Many native-born Americans hated the changes they saw around them and wanted to blame somebody. The Italian immigrants, who were the largest and most recently arrived ethnic group and whose language and customs seemed strange, were the perfect targets. In big cities with high immigrant populations, ethnic groups who had arrived earlier feared that the Italians would take their jobs and drive wages down, because the Italians were used to working for less.

Hostility toward Italian Americans took many forms. Newspapers criticized them in editorials, schoolboys taunted them in the streets, and politicians called for restrictions on immigration. One woman remembered American-born children throwing snowballs at her whenever she left her home in the winter, and shouting, "Guinea! Guinea!" an ethnic slur commonly used against Italians.

Some of the prejudice against Italian Americans manifested itself in small ways that were nonetheless painful, and it started at a young age. Michael A. Musmanno, who was elected in 1952 to the Supreme Court of Pennsylvania, describes one such incident from his childhood:

> I was born in Pennsylvania, but it was assumed that did not make me American, since my father and mother were born in Italy. . . . At twelve years of age I fell in love with a very pretty girl [named Penelope Worthington] who had recently arrived from England. . . . It was

"What Shall We Do with the Dago?"

The victims of the biggest mass lynching in U.S. history were Italian Americans. It occurred in 1891 in New Orleans. Animosity toward Italians had been growing there, fueled by the anxiety of Irish American fishermen. Used to running the waterfront, the Irish feared that the increasing Sicilian-born population would take work from them. (Almost all the Italian Americans in New Orleans at the time were from Sicily.) That fear escalated into mistrust and suspicion against Italians throughout the city. Eventually, the anti-Italian sentiment culminated in the New Orleans Massacre, a tragedy that prompted one national magazine to ask in a headline, "What Shall We Do with the Dago?"

On October 15, 1890, a controversial police chief, David Hennessy, was mortally wounded by unknown assailants. Before he died, Hennessy revealed that "dagoes" (Italians) shot him. The outraged police force lashed out. Officers swept through the city, rounding up Italian Americans. They arrested three hundred Italian Americans even though they had no evidence against them. All but nineteen of the suspects were eventually released, some after lengthy interrogations. The remaining nineteen faced a trial in February 1891, eleven of them accused as murderers and the other eight as accessories. At the trial, the presiding judge threw out the charges against some of the defendants. The jury acquitted the rest.

An outraged mob of five thousand men, however, took matters into its own hands, shooting some of the eleven exonerated Italians and hanging the rest. From nearby balconies, people watched the riot through opera glasses.

Although New Orleans society and many prominent Americans condoned the lynchings, much of the nation reacted with horror. Europe was even less forgiving. Italy responded by withdrawing its diplomatic representative to the United States. There was even talk of war between the two countries. Eventually the U.S. government paid reparations to the victims' families. No member of the mob ever faced trial for the eleven murders.

not long until I was accompanying her home, carrying her books, and writing her notes of devotion. One day I realized that when I grew up, Penelope Worthington should be my wife. . . . I felt rather timid about popping the question myself, so I got my boyhood chum, Arthur Young, to deliver the message. The next day, while the school bell was ringing, he reported. "Mike," he said, "I talked to Penelope and she said she loves you, she thinks you're wonderful and smart and she likes to listen to you talk. But she says she can never marry you because you're a foreigner."

I was born in America; she had been here seven months. [Yet] she was an American; I was a foreigner. The school bell seemed to be tolling my funeral. I did not even attempt to argue the question with her because I accepted what everybody said and believed. Italians were foreigners.[58]

Another successful Italian American politician, Fiorello LaGuardia, felt the weight of ethnic stereotyping at a young age, and cringed under the epithet "dago," a derogatory slang term for Italians. Say authors Mangione and Morreale, "He was ten years old when an organ grinder with a monkey came to his Arizona town and his friends began to tease him. 'I can still hear the cries of the kids,' he wrote fifty-six years later. 'Dago with a monkey! Hey, Fiorello, you're a Dago, too. Where's the monkey?' To make matters worse, his father came along, began chatting with the organ grinder, and wound up inviting him home for some macaroni.

'The kids taunted me for a long time after that.'"[59]

An Isolated Upbringing

For many children of immigrants, growing up in Little Italy provided little exposure to non-Italians. When they were finally cast into the larger world, many were shocked by the bias against them. One of these was Michael D'Innocenzo, a history professor who grew up in an Italian enclave. He says,

For me the shocker was when I left the ethnic neighborhood and went to col-

Many children of Italian immigrants had little exposure to the life and culture of non-Italians.

lege, and all of a sudden I was thrown into a situation where there was almost no one of Italian American background. . . . And people would call me greaser, wop, dago [derogatory terms for Italian Americans]. They didn't always mean it with hostility, but that was their characterization. It was the first time I felt in a minority. And it wasn't very pleasant.[60]

Language problems exacerbated the feeling of alienation. Many immigrants never learned to speak English, and some forced their children to speak Italian at home in order to keep the culture alive in the family. Retaining their language—and even the distinctive dialects of their home villages—helped the immigrants feel a connection with their neighbors and their distant homeland. But it also contributed to native-born Americans' perceptions of them as foreign and inscrutable. Because most Americans could not understand the Italian immigrants' language, they had no way of getting to know them personally, making it easier for the non-Italians to hang on to the insulting stereotypes and groundless accusations constantly leveled at the immigrants. In some U.S. schools, children who could not speak English were assumed to be "defective" and placed in classes for children with mental disabilities. Their placement in these slower-moving classes held them back academically and socially, and the label created a stigma that made it difficult for them to move ahead with their educations.

Scabs

As tension levels rose during the late nineteenth century, prejudice began erupting into

Although Italians' failure to learn English helped them feel connected to each other, it also held them back academically and socially.

violence. A recession in the 1870s marked the beginning of clashes between newly arrived southern Italian immigrants and the Irish laborers who had come to America earlier. In 1873, the city of New York passed a resolution asking the police department to show why Italian Americans had been hired for public works projects instead of Irish Americans.

The underlying problem was poverty. Until the Italian mass immigration, Irish Americans and recently freed slaves had occupied the bottom rungs of society's ladders. The new immigrants meant that more people were competing for the jobs available to unskilled workers. The Irish workers lashed out at the new arrivals because they were afraid the Italians would take their jobs. By the turn of the twentieth century, rapid industrialization created more jobs and eased some of the tensions between the two minority groups.

But until then, people who already had little were desperately afraid of losing everything.

This was a period of labor unrest. Exploited, dissatisfied workers in the lowest-level jobs sometimes went out on strike in an attempt to gain better wages or improved working conditions. When they walked out, management hired replacement workers, called "scabs," to fill in until the strike ended. Striking workers despised the scabs, whose presence kept the factories or mines operating, so management had little incentive to negotiate a fair deal with the strikers. Italian Americans, with their lack of English language skills and their willingness to work under any circumstances, made perfect scabs. They never asked why they'd been hired. Their padroni told them to work, so they worked. Later, as more Italian workers learned English, many would become labor leaders themselves. But before 1900, few understood enough English even to know they were breaking a strike.

In 1874, striking Irish workers in several cities violently attacked Italian replacement workers. The fervor against Italian Americans spilled over from striking Irish American laborers to other segments of the population, and in several cities, anti-Italian riots ensued. Between 1874 and 1915, mob violence killed dozens of Italian Americans and drove hundreds more from their homes.

Italians as Scapegoats

Violent crime was also on the rise in U.S. cities, and Irish Americans and others sought a scapegoat, someone to blame whether guilty or not. They found one in the mass of new immigrants. Thus, it was during the 1870s that Italians began to be stereotyped as criminals. Unfounded rumors said that the Italian government was sending its criminals to the United States, and American newspapers reported those rumors until many people, spurred by their desire to blame someone for the nation's problems, believed them. In response, the Italian-language newspaper *L'Eco d'Italia* pointed out in 1880 that most of the inmates in New York City's jails were Irish or native-born Americans, not Italians. But only Italians could read the article, and other newspapers ignored the story.

In fact, many reports and editorials in English-language newspapers only helped to entrench the popular stereotypical views of Italians. In 1888, an article in the *North American Review* argued that recent European immigrants, including Italians, were semibarbarians. Even the venerable *New York Times* blasted the immigrants, declaring in 1891, "These sneaking and cowardly Sicilians, the descendants of bandits and assassins, who had transported to this country the lawless passions, the cut-throat practices, the oath-bound societies of their native country, are to us a pest without mitigation."[61]

Antisocialist Sentiment

After the turn of the twentieth century, anti-Italian prejudice didn't focus as much on fears about job security as it did on Italian Americans as a political threat. World War I and the 1917 Russian Revolution left some Americans frightened of socialists, anarchists, and other proponents of left-wing political philosophies. They blamed such philosophies for the war in Europe and the revolution that had tossed aside a centuries-old Russian dynasty, and they wanted to avoid similar turmoil in the United States.

During the 1920s, the new leaders in Italy hated socialism even more than mainstream America did. Italian socialists faced government persecution; the regime would arrest and even execute them for speaking their views. As a result, many Italian socialists escaped to the United States. Although their numbers were few, the presence of these political refugees led to a stereotype of all Italian Americans as being radicals, including socialists (who believe that all people should collectively own the means of producing and distributing goods) and anarchists (who oppose all forms of organized government). Some Italian immigrants actually were socialists or anarchists, but most were not.

The U.S. labor movement—a system that helped workers band together to force companies to treat them fairly—had long been associated, sometimes accurately, with socialism. Gradually, as Italian workers improved their language skills and learned more about their new homeland, they began to realize how badly some employers were exploiting them. As greenies, they had accepted their American wages as a princely sum, compared to what they had made in the vineyards of Calabria or the sulfur mines of Sicily. But as experienced Italian Americans, they discovered just how low those wages were. After watching friends and relatives die in mine collapses and industrial accidents, the Italian Americans also understood how needlessly dangerous their jobs were. And despite their earlier conflicts with Irish laborers, more and more Italian Americans began taking on leadership roles in U.S. labor organizations, thus reinforcing common perceptions of Italians as radicals.

The Case of Sacco and Vanzetti

By 1920, a general antiradical hysteria had gripped the nation, and much of it targeted Americans of Italian birth or descent. In April of that year, robbers murdered two employees at a Massachusetts shoe factory. Authorities arrested and charged two Italian-born American citizens, Nicola Sacco and Bartolomeo Vanzetti, with the crime. Both were articulate, well-read working-class men who happened to be anarchists. Fearing them for that reason, many Americans had no interest in whether they'd actually committed the crimes.

The defendants insisted on their innocence. But they faced a trial before a judge who was openly hostile to Italians and a bigoted and biased jury foreman. According to Michael Musmanno, who was part of Sacco and Vanzetti's legal team, the foreman "always referred to Italians as dagoes. He also made the remark . . . that 'if he had the power' he would 'keep them out of the country.' Before hearing a word of testimony in the case he said to a friend: 'Damn them [Sacco and

Nicola Sacco (left) and Bartolomeo Vanzetti were found guilty of murder even though there was no real evidence against them.

Vanzetti]; they ought to hang anyway!'" The judge was also prejudiced against the defendants, says Musmanno: "Off the bench he referred to them as 'anarchistic bastards' and said that he would 'get them good and proper.'"[62] No credible evidence of the men's guilt was presented, but Sacco and Vanzetti were found guilty and sentenced to death.

For six years they appealed the sentence to higher courts, but to no avail. Supporters rallied to their cause, protesting widely in both the United States and Europe. "I am suffering because I am a radical and indeed I am a radical," declared Vanzetti at the sentencing. "I have suffered because I was an Italian, and indeed I am an Italian."[63] In August 1927, Sacco and Vanzetti were executed.

"A Cause for Serious Alarm"

Amid this atmosphere of rising xenophobia, or antiforeign sentiment, Congress took steps during the early 1920s to limit the number of immigrants allowed into the United States. Senator John K. Shields of Tennessee pushed hard for the restrictions, claiming that the immigrants of the twentieth century were different from those of the nineteenth, and were a "cause for serious alarm." He argued that the new immigrant groups, with heavy representation from Italy and other southern European countries, endangered "the purity of the blood, the homogeneity, and the supremacy of the American people." He said American citizenship would be "diluted, mongrelized, and destroyed"[64] if the nation continued to accept the new immigrants, leading to the demise of American society. Other legislators supported his views.

This attitude resulted in the Immigration Act of 1924, which all but stopped the flow of Italian immigrants into the United States. One writer claims that the act was intended to portray the United States as a "white-Anglo-

An American Icon Goes to War

New York Yankees baseball player Joe DiMaggio, the son of Sicilian-born parents, was already a national hero in the ballpark when he and two of his brothers left to fight for the United States in World War II. Despite his patriotism, wartime anti-Italian restrictions—which grew out of a 1941 presidential proclamation—limited his parents' freedom of movement. As Italian-born U.S. residents who had never become citizens, Giuseppe and Rosalie DiMaggio were prohibited from stepping onto a boat or even entering the Fisherman's Wharf district of San Francisco.

The DiMaggios had lived in the United States for forty years. They had worked hard all their lives, raising nine children on the meager wages of a San Francisco bait fisherman. Suddenly, despite their son's status as an American icon, and despite the fact that their sons were away fighting for the United States, the DiMaggios were considered foreigners. As long as the restrictions were in place, they couldn't continue working at their fishing business, and they were even prohibited from eating at the wharf restaurant owned by their famous son.

Most Italian Americans supported the fight against Italy during World War II.

Saxon-Protestant civilization somehow fighting against hordes of 'foreign' or 'colored' elements which threaten to destroy its pristine purity."[65]

The new law set a quota of 5,645 Italian immigrants per year, a tenth of the number that entered the country in 1924, the last year under the old system. In contrast, Great Britain was allowed 65,361 immigrants, even though only about 30,000 British residents had been immigrating to the United States each year.

Italian Americans in World War II

With the new quota in effect, the floodgates of immigration snapped shut. But immigrants already in the country still faced hostility from their adopted nation. Between 1941 and 1945, the United States and its allies fought in World War II against Germany and its allies, Japan and Italy. Italian Americans felt torn about fighting against their homeland. But virtually all acted with loyalty to their new country; no Italian

American was ever convicted of sabotage during the war. In fact, more Italians than any other ethnic group fought for the U.S. military. Some estimates put the number of Italian Americans at 1.5 million, a tenth of all U.S. forces.

Meanwhile, at home, Italian-born Americans who were not yet U.S. citizens faced groundless fears about their loyalty. On December 7, 1941, a Japanese attack on Pearl Harbor, Hawaii, plunged the United States into the war. The following day, U.S. president Franklin D. Roosevelt signed a presidential proclamation titled "Alien Enemies—Italians." The document declared Italian-born Americans who were not yet citizens to be enemies of the United States, and it granted the president the authority to incarcerate them during wartime without a trial. Roosevelt justified his actions because, as he stated in the proclamation, "an invasion of predatory incursion [a hostile invasion] is threatened upon the territory of the United States by Italy."[66]

The War at Home

Suddenly, immigrants who in some cases had been in the United States for more than half a century faced arduous limits on their freedom simply because their ethnicity made them suspect. Altogether, the new measures restricted the freedom of more than 600,000 Italian immigrants. Under a set of rules spearheaded by the FBI's J. Edgar Hoover and approved by Roosevelt, noncitizen, Italian-born immigrants had to be indoors between eight o'clock in the evening and eight o'clock in the morning. They had to carry special identification cards. They could not travel without authorization, and they were not allowed at

all in certain designated areas, including military installations and restricted zones along the coastlines—even if they lived or worked in those places. This rule forced ten thousand Italian Americans from their homes and caused others to lose their jobs. Italian-born Americans were also prohibited from boarding boats and airplanes. They couldn't own guns, cameras, or radios.

That last restriction caused Ralph De-Ricci's older sister Philomena, called Fanny, to rush to qualify for U.S. citizenship, rather than give up her radio. She had lived in the United States for thirty years, since childhood, and suddenly found herself branded an alien enemy. "They were taking radios away from all Italians who weren't U.S. citizens," says DeRicci's daughter, Carol Tomas. "You weren't allowed to have a radio. So she [Fanny] became a citizen so she could keep her radio."[67] German- and Japanese-born Americans faced the same restrictions.

Fisherman's Wharf, in San Francisco, was one of the areas to which Italians were denied access. That and the ban on being aboard boats nearly grounded the northern California seafood industry to a halt, since most San Francisco fishing families were Italian or Japanese.

Authorities enforced the rules more strictly on the West Coast than in the East, in part because the sheer numbers of Italians in the East would have made complete enforcement impossible. Another reason was the hard-nosed attitude of Lieutenant General John DeWitt, who headed up the Fourth Army and Western Defense Command in San Francisco. DeWitt's responsibilities included overseeing enforcement of the restrictions on the West Coast. And he believed fervently that the fifty thousand Italian-born California residents who had not become U.S. citizens were quietly awaiting orders from Rome to launch an attack against the United States.

The Camps

In 1941, President Roosevelt was asked if he planned to intern Italian Americans in relocation camps, where they would be kept isolated from the general population. Roosevelt replied, "I'm not worried about Italians. They're just a bunch of opera singers."[68]

That same year, he changed his mind at the urging of FBI chief Hoover, however, who believed the Italians constituted a real threat to national security. The United States seized between three thousand and four thousand

---

"My Golly, They Kidnap Me!"

When Italy entered World War II against the United States, many Americans—including some at high levels of government—feared acts of espionage from Italians living in the United States, even though most had been in the country for decades. There was no evidence that anyone of Italian background intended to sabotage the nation's war effort. Still, President Franklin Roosevelt instituted measures that drastically restricted the rights of Italian-born U.S. residents. In 1942, the authorities began arresting some Italian Americans and placing them in detention camps as a precautionary measure. Stephen Fox's book *The Unknown Internment* tells the story in the words of the people who lived through it.

Joe Cervetto was one of those people. Cervetto immigrated to the United States in 1933. During World War II, he was the president of a window washers' association. One evening as he sat down to dinner with his wife and daughter, FBI agents knocked on his door and ordered him to come with them, taking no possessions.

"I thought, 'My golly, they kidnap me!'" Cervetto told Fox. "I didn't know anything. I couldn't say anything. . . . I told the guy, 'I didn't have any dinner; I was just starting to eat.' 'Well,' he said, 'forget it. Tomorrow you get a breakfast.'"

The next morning, Cervetto and fifty other Italian- and German-born detainees were taken to Angel Island in San Francisco Bay. There they were interrogated. "They asked me constantly, 'Are you a Fascist?' I wasn't. I said, 'Look, my mother always told me that if you tell the truth you don't have anything to worry about.' But every day they asked me the same damned question, and I said the same thing."

Cervetto's wife, who was an American citizen, intervened with an FBI agent she knew, and eventually her husband was released. But first he was transferred to another internment camp, this one at Sharp Park, in Pacifica, California. "It was surrounded by barbed wire," said Cervetto. "No barbed wire on Angel Island."

Italian-born residents and incarcerated them in camps located throughout the country. Only men were locked up because men were considered the most dangerous.

Missoula, Montana, had the largest of these camps. One of the prisoners there was Venetian-born Al Cipolato, who in 1941 had been serving food in the Italian pavilion of the World's Fair in New York. Authorities sent him first to a Miami jail and then to a makeshift internment center set up on Ellis Island before sending him by train to Montana.

Cipolato remembers conditions for the prisoners in Missoula as generally good, although losing their families and their free-doms was hard for the detainees. Cipolato made the best of the situation, however:

Life in Montana was calm and the food excellent, even though the camp was surrounded by a high wire fence and guards. There was a beautiful library, tennis courts, and other athletic facilities. We were never bothered. . . . I think there must have been about one thousand Italians there. . . . After seventeen months, thirteen of [us] were released to cut sugar beets just outside the city limits. They took us to the fields by truck with more guards and machine guns

During World War II, the U.S. government forced some Italian-born men to move to relocation camps, leaving their families to fend for themselves.

than prisoners. When we said we would not work under such conditions they agreed to take us back and forth without heavy guard. . . . Later they sent us to Gold Creek, Montana . . . also to cut sugar beets, where we lived in a huge chicken barn. We made the place livable by first cleaning it, then hanging sheets for curtains and making a table.[69]

Most of the Italian detainees were incarcerated for less than a year. By the middle of 1943, the government, having found no evidence of espionage among Italian Americans, finally released the prisoners. In the fall of 2000, both houses of the U.S. Congress passed the Wartime Violation of Italian American Civil Liberties Act. The bill states as its purpose, "to provide for the preparation of a Government report detailing injustices suffered by Italian Americans during World War II, and a formal acknowledgment of such injustices by the President."[70] The text of the bill admits that the violations of Italian Americans' rights have never been acknowledged by the federal government, and that much of the information on the injustices is still classified, nearly sixty years later.

Overcoming Prejudice

Time and time again, Italian Americans fought discrimination in their new land and overcame it. They worked hard to gain acceptance into American society. Along the way, they faced verbal abuse, insulting stereotypes, and physical violence from those who saw them as too alien to fit in. Their own dogged persistence, their gradually increasing savvy about life in the United States, and their growing acceptance of American customs and the English language helped the immigrants prove themselves to longtime Americans, who began to see that they weren't so alien after all.

EPILOGUE

Blending Old and New

As Italian Americans became accustomed to their new lives in the United States, they began to make sense of—and make use of—the social, political, and cultural institutions around them while still holding on to some traditional Italian values and customs. Some saints' feast celebrations have remained basically unchanged since the days of mass immigration. Little Italy sections of major cities throughout the United States still steep residents and visitors in authentic Italian food, merchandise, and culture. And many Italians still live in the cities and neighborhoods their parents and grandparents immigrated to, often alongside the descendants of others from the same Italian hill towns.

Literacy and Upward Mobility

At the same time, Italian Americans have adapted other values and customs from their homeland to fit the new world in which they found themselves. For example, many immigrants came from a southern Italian tradition in which illiteracy was the norm. Education was seen as a selfish endeavor that kept children from contributing their share to the family finances. Second- and third-generation Italian Americans, though, tended to cast off that attitude in favor of the preparation to allow their children upward mobility. And that mobility has reached into the highest levels of American society.

Geraldine Ferraro, the first woman and the first Italian American to run for U.S. vice president on a national ticket, recalls helping her mother answer an admitting nurse's questions at the hospital:

[The nurse] said to my mother, "Did you graduate from high school?" And my mother said no. And then my mother said, "But I graduated from elementary school. . . ." I will never forget; she was sitting there with her hands on her lap, and she looked at me and here's what she said: "Big deal, huh?" And I felt so bad for her. . . . I was so devastated. . . . I put my arms around her and I said, "You'd better believe it's a big deal. You tell me any other person in this country . . . who has graduated from Harvard, Princeton, Yale—any of these great schools, with as many degrees as you want—any one of them who can say, 'My daughter ran for vice president of the United States.'"[71]

All Americans can now enjoy authentic Italian foods, merchandise, and culture.

Moving into Public Service

From a people once criticized for their lack of political involvement, Italian Americans have evolved into some of the most influential politicians and social leaders in America. John Orlando Pastore in 1945 became Rhode Island's first Italian American governor. Five years later, he became the first Italian American elected to the U.S. Senate, where he served until 1976. As early as the 1940s, both San Francisco and New York City had Italian mayors. In 1962, President John F. Kennedy appointed Cleveland mayor Anthony Celebrezze, a southern Italian native, as U.S. secretary of Health, Education, and Welfare. And New Jersey–born Antonin Scalia, a Sicilian American, sits on the Supreme Court, where he has been acknowledged as an influential leader of the Court's conservative justices.

More than anywhere else, though, New York provided Italian Americans with a forum for political expression. From the earliest years of the twentieth century, voters there were electing Italians as state legislators, congressmen, and judges. New York voters embraced Italian politicians to such an extent that, in 1950, all three candidates for New York City mayor were Italian.

A New Mind-Set Toward Law Enforcement

The fact that Italian immigrants would aspire to public office in America shows how far they had come from their Mezzogiorno roots. In preunification Italy, peasants mistrusted the police, who were employed by the rich landowners to strong-arm the poor and intimidate them into following orders.

The *contadini* carried that mind-set with them across the Atlantic, trusting each other and even the corrupt padroni rather than turning to police and other U.S. authorities for help. In addition, Irish Americans dominated the police departments of many major east-

Geraldine Ferraro (right), with 1984 presidential candidate Walter Mondale, was the first Italian American and the first woman to run for U.S. vice president on a national ticket.

The "Little Flower" of New York

Fiorello LaGuardia is remembered as an eccentric but effective mayor of New York City. For decades before his election, though, he was an important political thinker, an aggressive champion of the rights of all Americans, and a reformer who sought to improve the system from within.

The son of a southern Italian musician who moved to the United States in 1880 and joined the U.S. Army as a bandmaster in Arizona, Fiorello (the name means "Little Flower"), born in 1882, experienced ethnic hostility from a young age, when the other children called him a dago. He left home at age fifteen to be a newspaper correspondent in the Mexican War. Later, he worked as an interpreter at Ellis Island. Appalled at the treatment of newly arriving immigrants, LaGuardia went to law school and developed a practice in immigration law. He charged $10 a case, but only if the defendant could pay. For others, he worked for free.

LaGuardia spent time as a labor organizer and as deputy attorney general for New York before his election to Congress in 1916. A year later, during a debate on instituting the draft (for World War I), one of the opposing representatives asked caustically how many members of the House who were voting to send boys to war would go themselves. LaGuardia was one of five who stood up. Soon afterward, he enlisted in the Air Corps.

Back in Congress after the war, he unsuccessfully fought against a resurgence of racist attitudes that culminated in new limits on immigration, but he was more successful in his efforts to safeguard workers' rights. His major legislative achievement was the Norris-LaGuardia Anti-Injunction Act, signed by President Herbert Hoover in 1932, which established the right of workers to bargain collectively. In 1933, after fourteen years in Congress, LaGuardia became mayor of New York City, where he was known as a liberal firebrand who stood up for the rights of Italian immigrants and other working-class people.

ern cities around the turn of the twentieth century, and the longstanding rivalry between the two ethnic groups made cooperation difficult.

Tensions eased gradually, though, as jobs proved plentiful and as Italian immigrants gained English skills, education, and savvy in the ways of their new country. Eventually, they became confident enough in their new surroundings to develop some level of trust in the institutions of the United States, including the police departments. In fact, Italian Americans ended up filling key law enforcement positions throughout the country. The man who pursued outlaws Billy the Kid, Butch Cassidy, and the Sundance Kid, for instance, was Italian-born Charlie Angelo Siringo, a detective and chronicler of the Wild West. Before becoming mayor of

New York City, Rudolph Giuliani spent twenty-five years fighting crime for the U.S. Department of Justice. Even the founder of the Federal Bureau of Investigation, Charles J. Bonaparte, was of Italian lineage.

New Customs for a New World

Learning to trust authority figures was difficult enough for the immigrants. But to integrate fully into their new surroundings, Italian Americans had to change an even more entrenched mind-set they had carried across the ocean from their southern hill towns: They had to learn to relax the sometimes rigid gender roles imposed on men and women in the Old Country. Once immigrants moved to the United States, arranged marriages quickly fell out of favor. Although the older Italians still pushed for arranged marriages, young people balked at being forced to marry someone chosen for them. In Italy they might have

Italian American Rudolph Giuliani worked for the U.S. Department of Justice before being elected mayor of New York City.

had no recourse but to go along. In the United States, however, they couldn't be forced to marry against their will.

Another big difference was that Italian women began taking a more visible role in affairs outside their own homes. In nineteenth-century Italy, a wife was supposed to defer to her husband's wishes in all things, even though the harsh life and hard work of the Mezzogiorno created women who were strong and in command. "Tough" is a word that comes up again and again when the children of immigrants describe their mothers. Often it was the women who made the decisions for their households, but outside the house, they pretended to follow their husbands' leads so as not to embarass their men. In the United States, especially after women gained the right to vote in 1920, Italian American women began to have more freedom. They no longer had to hide their interests and abilities and gradually began to enter politics themselves, pursue careers, and openly work for social change.

In fact, Eleanor Cutri Smeal, who was elected president of the National Organization for Women in 1970, is the daughter of a Calabrian father who immigrated after nearly being killed in a 1909 Italian earthquake. Smeal's mother, whose family came from Naples, always urged her to stand up for her rights, in stark contrast to the advice Italian mothers had given their daughters back in the hill towns of the Mezzogiorno. "You only live one life," Smeal's mother told her. "Why should you be cheated?"[72]

All Fields of Endeavor

The descendants of Italian immigrants, women and men alike, have moved into fields their parents and grandparents could never have imagined. Although some Italian Americans still pick vegetables, protect beloved fig trees from the cold, and nurture grapevines, most have moved out of agriculture and into other areas of achievement, including the sciences, medicine, education, and business. Probably the most famous Italian American business leader is Lee Iacocca, who revived the ailing U.S. car manufacturer Chrysler during the 1980s. And around the turn of the twentieth century, Amedeo Obici and Mario Peruzzi, two immigrants in Wilkes-Barre, Pennsylvania, created the Planters Peanut Company and its well-loved "Mr. Peanut" logo. By 1930, the partners had four plants and sales of $12 million a year.

As popular music changed over the years, Italian opera singers gave way to Italian crooners like Frank Sinatra and Perry Como, who have in turn given way to more recent Italian American pop and rock music stars such as Madonna, Sonny Bono, and Jon Bon Jovi. In the last few decades, such recording artists have proven to have mainstream appeal, attracting audiences that for the most part are not of Italian descent.

La Storia Continues

In very small numbers, Italian immigration continues today. In 1998, according to U.S. Immigration and Naturalization Service reports, about two thousand Italians were admitted into the United States. The flight of agriculture workers from Italy is long gone, however. Most of the 1998 immigrants who listed occupations said they were professional and technical specialists, managers, and service workers.

Jon Bon Jovi is one of several Italian American music stars who have reached mainstream audiences.

But most Italian Americans and others agree that the stories of all Italian immigrants, past and present, need to be told and remembered. Professor Michael D'Innocenzo recounts how his immigrant father urged him to keep the story alive:

> When I became a history teacher . . . he kept saying, "Miguel, you're a big shot! When are you going to write about *my* story?" And as so often happens when it's close to your family, I kept putting it off; I figured there was no rush.

> My father was seventy-three at the time. And he finally really pressured me to tape-record and interview him. And I did. I had him talk about his own experience. And when we were through I said to him. . . . "What do you want to call your story?" I'll never forget. He looked at me and said, "Miguel, you call it How the Low People Moved Up."[73]

NOTES

Introduction: A New Odyssey

1. Quoted in Luciano J. Iorizzo and Salvatore Mondello, *The Italian-Americans*. Boston: Twayne, 1971, p. 48.

Chapter 1: Roots of Mass Migration

2. Quoted in Iorizzo and Mondello, *The Italian-Americans*, p. 42.
3. Gay Talese, *Unto the Sons*. New York: Knopf, 1992, p. 296.
4. Quoted in Jerre Mangione and Ben Morreale, *La Storia: Five Centuries of the Italian American Experience*. New York: HarperCollins, 1992, p. 68.
5. Mangione and Morreale, *La Storia*, p. 60.
6. Booker T. Washington, with Robert E. Park, *The Man Farthest Down: A Record of Observation and Study in Europe*. New York: Doubleday, 1912, p. 144.
7. Talese, *Unto the Sons*, p. 50.
8. Mangione and Morreale, *La Storia*, p. 51.
9. Michael A. Musmanno, *The Story of the Italians in America*. Garden City, NY: Doubleday, 1965, p. 195.
10. Mangione and Morreale, *La Storia*, p. 51.

Chapter 2: The Decision to Leave

11. Quoted in Ben Morreale and Robert Carola, *Italian Americans: The Immigrant Experience*. Southport, CT: Hugh Lauter Levin, 2000, p. 54.
12. Erik Amfitheatrof, *The Children of Columbus: An Informal History of Italians in the New World*. Boston: Little, Brown, 1973, pp. 156–57.

13. Quoted in *The Italian Americans* video program, produced and written by Sam Toperoff. Plainview, NY: WLIW21 Public Television, 1997.
14. Quoted in Iorizzo and Mondello, *The Italian-Americans*, p. 47.
15. Ralph DeRicci, interviews with the author, Peckville, PA, and Burke, VA, August 1999–April 2001.
16. Mary Ciabocchi, telephone interview with the author, Old Forge, PA, March 2001.
17. Talese, *Unto the Sons*, p. 249.

Chapter 3: Atlantic Crossing

18. Quoted in Mangione and Morreale, *La Storia*, p. 87.
19. Morreale and Carola, *Italian Americans*, p. 63.
20. Quoted in David M. Brownstone, Irene M. Franck, and Douglass L. Brownstone, *Island of Hope, Island of Tears*. New York: Rawson, Wade, 1979, p. 33.
21. Quoted in Brownstone, Franck, and Brownstone, *Island of Hope, Island of Tears*, p. 109.
22. Quoted in Amfitheatrof, *The Children of Columbus*, p. 254.
23. Quoted in Dorothy and Thomas Hoobler, *The Italian American Family Album*. New York: Oxford University Press, 1994, p. 26.
24. Quoted in Hoobler and Hoobler, *The Italian American Family Album*, p. 28.
25. Quoted in Hoobler and Hoobler, *The Italian American Family Album*, p. 29.

Chapter 4: Welcome to America

26. Talese, *Unto the Sons*, pp. 396–97.
27. Quoted in Brownstone, Franck, and Brownstone, *Island of Hope, Island of Tears*, p. 180.
28. Quoted in Brownstone, Franck, and Brownstone, *Island of Hope, Island of Tears*, pp. 183–84.
29. Quoted in Pamela Reeves, *Ellis Island: Gateway to the American Dream*. New York: Barnes & Noble, 1998, p. 43.
30. Brownstone, Franck, and Brownstone, *Island of Hope, Island of Tears*, p. 166.
31. Morreale and Carola, *Italian Americans*, p. 82.

Chapter 5: On the Job in the United States

32. Quoted in *The Italian Americans* video.
33. Talese, *Unto the Sons*, p. 227.
34. Quoted in Iorizzo and Mondello, *The Italian-Americans*, p. 53.
35. Ciabocchi, interview with the author.
36. Quoted in Susan Campbell Bartoletti, *Growing Up in Coal Country*. Boston: Houghton Mifflin, 1996, p. 61.
37. Quoted in *The Italian Americans* video.
38. Quoted in Rose Musacchio Higdon and Hal Higdon, *Falconara: A Family Odyssey*. Michigan City, IN: Roadrunner Press, 1993, p. 100.
39. Edward A. D'Alessandro, *The Ginney Block: Reminiscences of an Italian-American Dead-End Street Kid*. Baltimore: Gateway Press, 1988, p. xi.
40. DeRicci, interview with the author.
41. Bartoletti, *Growing Up in Coal Country*, p. 13.
42. Quoted in Iorizzo and Mondello, *The Italian-Americans*, p. 21.
43. Quoted in *The Italian Americans* video.

Chapter 6: Creating Little Italy

44. Ciabocchi, interview with the author.
45. DeRicci, interview with the author.
46. Quoted in Amfitheatrof, *The Children of Columbus*, p. 165.
47. D'Alessandro, *The Ginney Block*, p. xiii.
48. Bartoletti, *Growing Up in Coal Country*, pp. 67–68.
49. Quoted in Howard Clifford, *Rails North: The Railroads of Alaska and the Yukon*. Seattle, WA: Superior Publishing, 1981, pp. 82–83.
50. Ciabocchi, interview with the author.
51. Bartoletti, *Growing Up in Coal Country*, p. 77.
52. Quoted in *The Italian Americans* video.
53. Vincent Schiavelli, *Bruculinu, America: Remembrances of Sicilian-American Brooklyn, Told in Stories and Recipes*. Boston: Houghton Mifflin, 1998, pp. 8–9.
54. Morreale and Carola, *Italian Americans*, p. 106.
55. Quoted in Amfitheatrof, *The Children of Columbus*, p. 196.
56. Quoted in *The Italian Americans* video.
57. Quoted in *The Italian Americans* video.

Chapter 7: Liberty's Broken Promise

58. Musmanno, *The Story of the Italians in America*, p. 7.
59. Quoted in Mangione and Morreale, *La Storia*, p. 189.
60. Quoted in *The Italian Americans* video.
61. Quoted in Iorizzo and Mondello, *The Italian-Americans*, p. 70.
62. Musmanno, *The Story of the Italians in America*, pp. 143–44.

63. Musmanno, *The Story of the Italians in America,* pp. 145.

64. Quoted in Musmanno, *The Story of the Italians in America,* p. 119.

65. Quoted in Musmanno, *The Story of the Italians in America,* p. 120.

66. Franklin D. Roosevelt, "Alien Enemies—Italians," *Presidential Proclamation No. 2527: Aliens,* December 8, 1941.

67. Carol A. Tomas, interview with the author, Burke, VA, 2001.

68. Quoted in Mangione and Morreale, *La Storia,* p. 25.

69. Quoted in Stephen Fox, *The Unknown Internment: An Oral History of the Relocation of Italian Americans During World War II.* Boston: Twayne, 1990, pp. 164–65.

70. Wartime Violation of Italian American Civil Liberties Act, 106th Congress, H.R. 2442, 1999.

Epilogue: Blending Old and New

71. Quoted in *The Italian Americans* video.

72. Quoted in Hoobler and Hoobler, *The Italian American Family Album,* p. 101.

73. Quoted in *The Italian Americans* video.

FOR FURTHER READING

J. Philip Di Franco, *The Italian Americans.* New York: Chelsea House, 1988. Part of "The Immigrant Experience" series, this volume discusses the history, culture, and religion of the Italians; factors that led to their immigration; and their acceptance into American society.

Kathleen Fahey, *The Italians.* St. Catharines, Ontario, Canada: Crabtree, 2000. At the height of emigration from Italy, children were recruited by padroni and brought to the United States to work as shoe shiners, musicians, and even acrobats. Part of the "We Came to North America" series, this account of how the Italians came to North America and how their traditions are still celebrated today is highlighted with full color artwork and eyewitness accounts.

Ronald P. Grossman, with Martha Savaglio, *Italians in America.* Minneapolis, MN: Lerner Publications, 1993. A discussion of the contributions that Italian explorers and immigrants made to the history and civilization of the United States.

Maria Laurino, *Were You Always an Italian?* New York: W. W. Norton, 2000. A series of thoughtful, penetrating, and sometimes funny essays that dismantles the stereotypes about growing up Italian in America.

Barbara Marinacci, *They Came from Italy: The Stories of Famous Italian Americans.* New York: Dodd, Mead, 1967. Profiles of extraordinary Italians in America, including philosopher and Thomas Jefferson adviser Philip Mazzei; war hero, amateur archaeologist, and museum curator Luigi Palma di Cesnola; maestro Arturo Toscanini; politician and social reformer Fiorello LaGuardia, "the biggest little man in America"; and more. Includes maps and illustrations.

Jim Murphy, *Pick and Shovel Poet.* New York: Clarion, 2000. The biography of an Italian peasant who immigrated to America in the early twentieth century and endured the difficult life of an unskilled laborer while determined to become a published poet.

Carl Sifakis, *The Mafia Encyclopedia: From Accardo to Zwillman.* New York: Facts On File, 1987. This reference book, written by a former crime reporter, provides a wealth of easy-to-read information about the criminal organization popularly known as the Mafia. Its four-hundred-plus entries include biographical essays of major mafiosi and crime fighters, definitions of terms related to organized crime, and descriptions of Mafia activities.

Jerry Spinelli, *Knots in My Yo-Yo String: The Autobiography of a Kid.* New York: Knopf, 1998. The story of the Italian American Newbery Award winner's childhood has all the warmth, humor, and drama of his best-selling fiction. Illustrated with photographs and a map.

WORKS CONSULTED

Books

Erik Amfitheatrof, *The Children of Columbus: An Informal History of Italians in the New World*. Boston: Little, Brown, 1973. A rich, detailed, and personal look at Italians in the New World, beginning with the early explorers and continuing through to mid–twentieth century. Includes a thorough discussion of the life and work of Fiorello LaGuardia.

Susan Campbell Bartoletti, *Growing Up in Coal Country*. Boston: Houghton Mifflin, 1996. A fascinating look at the children who worked in and around the coal mines of Pennsylvania around the start of the twentieth century. Danger, deprivation, and an occasional lighthearted moment, in and out of the mines, come to life through period photographs and personal recollections.

David M. Brownstone, Irene M. Franck, and Douglass L. Brownstone, *Island of Hope, Island of Tears*. New York: Rawson, Wade, 1979. This book contains first-person accounts and photographs of the people who immigrated to the United States through the Ellis Island entry port.

Howard Clifford, *Rails North: The Railroads of Alaska and the Yukon*. Seattle, WA: Superior Publishing, 1981. This illustrated history includes detailed information on the people and events that played a part in the building of the railroads across Alaska and Canada's Yukon territory.

Terence Cole, *Crooked Past: A History of a Frontier Gold Town*. Anchorage, AK: Alaska Northwest, 1984. The early twentieth-century gold-mining history of Fairbanks, Alaska, beginning with Felix Pedro and his discovery of gold there.

Mario Costantino and Lawrence Gambella, *The Italian Way: Aspects of Behavior, Attitudes, and Customs of the Italians*. Lincolnwood, IL: Passport, 1996. This slim volume provides an alphabetical guide to Italian customs and culture. It consists of brief, informative explanations of concepts such as *il campanilismo,* a strong attachment to one's village; celebrations and holidays; and the wines of Italy. Includes a bibliography and index.

Edward A. D'Alessandro, *The Ginney Block: Reminiscences of an Italian-American Dead-End Street Kid*. Baltimore: Gateway Press, 1988. A series of loosely connected remembrances of life in an Italian American enclave in Cleveland, told from the viewpoint of a boy growing up there in the early twentieth century.

Stephen Fox, *Blood and Power: Organized Crime in Twentieth-Century America*. New York: Morrow, 1989. A detailed history of the Mafia and other U.S. crime organizations, analyzing how and why organized crime took hold, taking into account ethnic, cultural, historical, and religious influences.

———, *The Unknown Internment: An Oral History of the Relocation of Italian Americans During World War II*. Boston: Twayne, 1990. Filled with firsthand accounts, this book describes the little-known U.S. government campaign to persecute and incarcerate Italian-born Americans during World War II because of unfounded fears of their collaboration with the enemy.

Rose Musacchio Higdon and Hal Higdon, *Falconara: A Family Odyssey*. Michigan City, IN: Roadrunner Press, 1993. Growing up in Chicago, Rose Musacchio heard stories of her ancestors, seven royal families who fled Albania in 1476 to escape Turkish invaders. They immigrated to southern Italy, where they founded the town of Falconara-Albanese. Generations later, descendants of these Albanian Italians immigrated to the United States. Their story and the authors' search for the truth about the family make up this unusual, fascinating, and highly personal narrative.

George Holmes, ed., *The Oxford History of Italy*. New York: Oxford University Press, 1997. An elegantly written and richly illustrated history of Italy from ancient times to the present.

Dorothy and Thomas Hoobler, *The Italian American Family Album*. New York: Oxford University Press, 1994. This succinct, entertaining account of Italians in America tells the stories of the ordinary and extraordinary people who have contributed to the culture of Italian America. Chock-full of photographs, it also contains profiles of famous Italian Americans and a helpful timeline.

Luciano J. Iorizzo and Salvatore Mondello, *The Italian-Americans*. Boston: Twayne, 1971. A detailed, well-researched, and objective account of Italian immigration and the problems immigrants have faced in the New World.

Salvatore J. Lagumina, Frank J. Cavaioli, Salvatore Primeggia, and Joseph A. Vara-

calli, eds., *The Italian American Experience: An Encyclopedia*. New York: Garland, 2000. This comprehensive reference to everything Italian American includes contributions from more than 150 scholars and plenty of photographs. It gives an objective account of the history, culture, and assimilation of Italians in the United States, from the colonial period to the present, and includes Italian Americans' role in the arts, politics, sports, and religion.

Frances M. Malpezzi and William M. Clements, *Italian-American Folklore*. Little Rock, AR: August House, 1992. A fun, well-researched look at the proverbs, songs, games, folk tales, food-related customs, superstitions, and folk remedies of Italian Americans.

Jerre Mangione and Ben Morreale, *La Storia: Five Centuries of the Italian American Experience*. New York: HarperCollins, 1992. A well-written, thorough, and highly readable history of Italians in the New World, from the Renaissance to modern times.

Ben Morreale and Robert Carola, *Italian Americans: The Immigrant Experience*. Southport, CT: Hugh Lauter Levin, 2000. Heavier on photographs than on scholarship, this beautifully illustrated large-format volume is nonetheless an excellent introduction to the experiences of Italian immigrants. It begins with a brief history of Italy and traces immigrants from their poverty-stricken hill towns to the cities and suburbs of America, including some fascinating sidebars that spotlight people and events.

Michael A. Musmanno, *The Story of the Italians in America*. Garden City, NY: Doubleday, 1965. Beginning with risorgimento, this highly personal history of

Italian immigration traces the achievements of Italian Americans through the mid–twentieth century. Includes particularly detailed accounts of the lives of Giuseppe Garibaldi and Fiorello LaGuardia, as well as extensive discussions of the arts.

Grant Pearson, *A History of Mount McKinley National Park*. Washington, DC: National Park Service, 1953. A history of Mount McKinley, or Denali, the highest peak in the United States, and the people who settled the Alaskan wilderness there.

Pamela Reeves, *Ellis Island: Gateway to the American Dream.* New York: Barnes & Noble, 1998. A nonscholarly but richly illustrated history of the main U.S. entry port for millions of Italians and other immigrants.

Vincent Schiavelli, *Bruculinu, America: Remembrances of Sicilian-American Brooklyn, Told in Stories and Recipes.* Boston: Houghton Mifflin, 1998. The Italian American character actor tells stories from his family's life in the Italian section of Brooklyn in the first half of the twentieth century, with a special emphasis on food. Includes dozens of recipes and mail-order information for Italian foods.

Rinn S. Shinn, ed., *Italy: A Country Study*. Washington, DC: U.S. Government Printing Office, 1985. A dry but detailed account of Italian history, with special information on government, economics, and national security.

David and Brenda Stone, *Hard Rock Gold: The Story of the Great Mines That Were the Heartbeat of Juneau*. Juneau, AK: Juneau Centennial Committee, 1980. A fascinating, illustrated history of mining in southeastern Alaska, including accounts of the work and lifestyles of the people who labored in the mines.

Gay Talese, *Unto the Sons*. New York: Knopf, 1992. Talese's ambitious autobiography is really the autobiography of a culture. He alternates recollections of his own life with accounts of his immigrant father's life and stories of his ancestors in the southern Italian village of Maida. Along the way he presents a well-researched history of Italian immigrants in America.

Bonnie Tiburzi, *Takeoff! The Story of America's First Woman Pilot for a Major Airline*. New York: Crown, 1984. The Italian American pilot describes her struggle to achieve her goal and the prejudices she faced before and after she made it.

Marianna DeMarco Torgovnick, *Crossing Ocean Parkway: Readings by an Italian American Daughter.* Chicago: University of Chicago Press, 1994. A well-written and personal series of essays centering on the clash between the author's Italian American background and the culture and expectations of mainstream America.

Booker T. Washington, with Robert E. Park, *The Man Farthest Down: A Record of Observation and Study in Europe.* New York: Doubleday, 1912. An account of the educator, reformer, and former slave's travels through Europe, with an extensive section on conditions in Italy.

Periodicals

Alvero Vito Beltroni, "Saga of Felix Pedro: His Find Launched the Camp," *Fairbanks Daily News-Miner,* July 20, 1967. (Reprinted from the *Gazetta Italiana*, July 18, 1952.)

E. W. Kenworthy, "Celebrezze Faces a New Kind of Job: Cleveland Mayor May

Find Cabinet Post Frustrating," *New York Times,* July 16, 1962.

Nancy S. Montgomery, "A Master Carver: Building for Eternity," *Cathedral Age,* Spring 2001.

Government Documents

Franklin D. Roosevelt, "Alien Enemies—Italians," *Presidential Proclamation No. 2527: Aliens,* December 8, 1941.

Statistical Yearbook of Immigration, 1998. Washington, DC: U.S. Government Printing Office, 2000.

Wartime Violation of Italian American Civil Liberties Act, 106th Congress, H.R. 2442, July 1, 1999.

Internet Sources

"American Names: Declaring Independence," *INS History, Genealogy, and Education.* Immigration and Naturalization Service, November 12, 1999. www.ins.usdoj.gov/graphics/aboutins/history/articles/NameEssay.html.

"Changing Immigrant Names," *INS History, Genealogy, and Education.* Immigration and Naturalization Service, November 11, 1999. www.ins.usdoj.gov/graphics/aboutins/history/articles/NAMES.html.

Michael J. Cochran, "Enrico Caruso," *Welcome to Tenorland.* www.geocities.com/Vienna/1450/caruso.htm.

"Fight Defamation and Promote Positive Images," *One Stop Italian America: Your Passsport to the Very Best of Italian America.* www.osia.org/public/htm.

"Marshall, Penny," *Women in American History by Encyclopaedia Britannica.* Britannica Online, 1999. http://women.eb.com/women/articles/Marshall_Penny.html.

Deborah K. Millemaci, "What's in a Name? Researching Our Italian Surnames," *Virtualitalia.com.* www.virtualitalia.com/gene/inaname.shtml.

Gregg Patruno, "The Messina-Reggio Earthquake: 1908," *Arduini & Pizzo Italian-American Family History Web Site.* www.arduini.net/tales/tales15a.htm.

Websites

Arduini & Pizzo: An Italian American Family History (www.arduini.net). This surprisingly thorough and comprehensive personal site includes fascinating, well-written family stories of life in the Old Country and the New World, both about the site owner's family and about other Italian Americans. Topics range from important events such as the Messina earthquake to intimate reminiscences of family life.

Embassy of Italy in the United States (www.italyemb.nw.dc.us). The Italian embassy's site contains fact sheets on subjects such as Italian history, government, economics, statistics, personalities, and travel.

Immigration and Naturalization Service (www.ins.gov). This agency—part of the U.S. Department of Justice—regulates, monitors, and manages immigration into the United States. In addition to forms and legal information for immigrating and becoming a U.S. citizen, the site provides historical and statistical data and includes a section on history, genealogy, and education.

The Italian Tribune (www.italiantribune.com). This Italian American weekly, founded in 1931, does not offer full text of the newspaper online. However, the nonetheless useful and entertaining site does include reports on topics of special interest to Italian Americans, selected editorials from the newspaper, and a recommended reading list.

National Archives and Records Administration (www.nara.gov). This government clearinghouse for historical information provides online versions of a wide variety of federal documents, a virtual tour of the archives' collection, information on available resources, and tips on how to do historical and genealogical research.

National Italian American Foundation (www.niaf.org). NIAF, the major advocate in Washington, D.C., for Italian Americans, works to preserve and protect Italian American heritage and culture. The website contains a wide variety of information on Italy and Italian Americans, including fact sheets on the achievements of Italian Americans in many fields, legislation affecting Italian Americans, reports on media stereotyping of Italian Americans, statistics, and reading lists.

Order Sons of Italy in America (www.osia.org). Founded in 1905, OSIA is the largest and longest-established Italian American organization. Its purpose is to enrich Italian heritage nationwide through programs in education, cultural preservation, grass-roots initiatives, charitable fund raising, and strengthening of ties between Italy and the United States. This wide-ranging site includes a section on culture and heritage, updates on legislation affecting Italian Americans, and reports on efforts to end negative stereotypes of Italian Americans in the media.

Film and Television

"Italian-American Internment: A Secret War," *History's Mysteries.* New York: History Channel, 1996. An exploration of the U.S. government's little-known incarceration of innocent Italian Americans during World War II. This fifty-minute program relies on archival footage, much of it formerly classified, as well as interviews with people who spent time in the relocation camps.

The Italian Americans, produced and written by Sam Toperoff. Plainview, NY: WLIW21 Public Television, 1997. This ninety-minute program provides a poignant, humorous, and entertaining overview of Italians in America. Through interviews and family film footage, it explores the bonds of family and community that enabled immigrant families to transplant their culture and values across an ocean. Italian American interview subjects include such prominent names as Tommy Lasorda, Geraldine Ferraro, and Joe Mantegna, as well as expert scholars and others.

Italians in America, written and directed by Laura Verklan. New York: History Channel, 1998. This portrait of the history and heritage of Italian Americans shares the stories of immigrants and their descendants through archival film footage and interviews with prominent Italian Americans, including Geraldine Ferraro and Gay Talese. Two videos, fifty minutes each.

"Joe DiMaggio: The Hero's Life," written by Richard Ben Cramer, *The American Experience.* Boston: WGBH, 2000. This ninety-minute program traces the journey of the Yankees' legendary baseball star, from his childhood as the son of hardworking Italian immigrants through his rise to nationwide celebrity as an athlete and his tumultuous marriage to actress Marilyn Monroe. Interviews include childhood chums, army pals, teammates, and family members.

"Rescue at Sea," written by Ben Loeterman, *The American Experience*. Boston: WGBH, 1999. This program tells the exciting story of the perilous 1909 collision between an Italian immigrant ship and an American luxury liner off the coast of Nantucket, Massachusetts, including the role of a new technological wonder, the wireless telegraph, in the successful midsea rescue of more than a thousand people.

INDEX

number of Italians who
immigrated to, 6–7,
23–24, 95
selling grain in Italy, 20
Unknown Internment, The
(Fox), 87
U.S. Capitol building, 63–64
U.S. Census Bureau, 7
U.S. Civil War, 20
U.S. Department of Justice, 94
U.S. Immigration and
Naturalization Services, 6, 95
U.S. Marine band, 76
U.S. Supreme Court, 92

Vanzetti, Bartolomeo, 83–84
Vatican, 13
Vecoli, Rudolph J., 11
Ventrasca, Francesco, 39
via dolorosa ("sorrowful

way"), 38, 41
Victor Emmanuel II, 13–16,
20, 22
villages, 70
vineyards, 20, 57
volcanoes, 20

Wartime Violation of Italian
American Civil Liberties
Act (2000), 89
Washington, Booker T., 16, 20
Washington, D.C., 63
wheat, 18, 20
white widows, 31
Williams, William Carlos, 46–47
wine, 20
World War I
Caruso raises money for
United States and Allies
during, 9

growing up in Italy during, 17
immigration of Italians
declines during, 7
Italian Americans as
political threats during,
82–83
LaGuardia enlists in Air
Corps, 93
steerage fares before, 41
World War II, 84–89
World's Fair (New York), 88
Worthington, Penelope,
79–80

xenophobia, 84

Yankees, 84
Young, Arthur, 80

zucchini, 77

PICTURE CREDITS

ABOUT THE AUTHOR

Catherine M. Petrini has written twenty young-adult novels, under pseudonyms, for "Sweet Valley High" and other teen series. Titles include *Wanted for Murder, A Stranger in the House, Mystery Date, Earthquake,* and a historical saga, *The Patmans of Sweet Valley.* A former magazine editor, she is also the coauthor of a nonfiction book, *Opportunities in Training and Development Careers.*

A frequent speaker on writing-related topics, Petrini also hosts a radio show. She has a bachelor's degree in English from the University of Virginia and a master's in writing from Johns Hopkins University.